Implementing
Patient Safety

Addressing Culture, Conditions, and
Values to Help People Work Safely

Implementing Patient Safety

Addressing Culture, Conditions, and Values to Help People Work Safely

By

Suzette Woodward

Routledge
Taylor & Francis Group

A PRODUCTIVITY PRESS BOOK

First edition published in 2020
by Routledge/Productivity Press
52 Vanderbilt Avenue, 11th Floor New York, NY 10017
2 Park Square, Milton Park, Abingdon, Oxon OX14 4RN, UK

© 2020 by Taylor & Francis Group, LLC
Routledge/Productivity Press is an imprint of Taylor & Francis Group, an Informa business

No claim to original U.S. Government works

Printed on acid-free paper

International Standard Book Number-13: 978-0-8153-7686-6 (Hardback)
International Standard Book Number-13: 978-0-8153-7685-9 (Paperback)
International Standard Book Number-13: 978-1-351-23538-9 (eBook)

Visit the Taylor & Francis website at
http://www.taylorandfrancis.com

Follow on from *Rethinking Patient Safety*

Dedicated to Dr Philip Woodward

1919–2018

While he is no longer with us, his impact
will echo beyond his time.

Contents

Preface

> The task is, not so much to see what no one has yet seen;
> but to think what nobody has yet thought, about that which
> everybody sees.
>
> **Schrodinger 1952**

Welcome to my second book *Implementing Patient Safety*.
This book builds on my first book, *Rethinking Patient Safety*
(Woodward 2017) which documented the thinking of leading
experts in safety and provided a few thoughts on what we
could do differently in healthcare in relation to safety. It was
called 'rethinking' patient safety because while patient safety
has widespread recognition across healthcare, and there have
been a number of developments which provide some hope,
there was a growing concern that the efforts of the last two
decades have not made the difference expected. This remains
the same today.

I have been studying safety in healthcare settings since the
1990s, predominantly in acute care settings and at a national
policy level. In retrospect, there are some fundamental things
I would have done differently and there are some things that
are blatantly wrong in the way we have tried to address safety
in healthcare. The first book, therefore, explored the prevailing approach to risk and safety and also highlighted the work

I was leading at the time in the Sign up to Safety campaign – a campaign for the National Health Service (NHS) in England which was designed to help create a safer system by focusing on culture and behaviours.

I have loved working in patient safety because it is endlessly fascinating. While pursuing my work I have studied all kinds of different aspects, including design, the impact of architecture and the colour of the walls on safety, the way in which pharmaceuticals and medical devices should be designed to make them intuitively safer, as well as behavioural change and social movements. Patient safety is so much more than incident reporting and incident investigations.

Throughout my safety career my main area of interest has been to translate theory, research, concepts and models into practice, to make it meaningful, relevant and understandable for everyone who works in healthcare. Part of this work has led me to a place I never thought I would be in studying safety. That is the world of joy, gratitude, kindness and wellbeing. I wanted to bring back the joy in safety, dispel the myths and provide some much-needed common sense.

This quest has led to this second book, *Implementing Patient Safety*. The aim of my second book is to take the ideas described in the first book, build on these and add a few more concepts and models to the mix and then help the reader think about how they could use them to help people who work in healthcare to do so as safely as they can. The book is also a lovely distillation of my thinking and that of many more who work in a variety of aspects of safety and beyond safety. I know I do not have all the answers and never will. I will always stay curious and own that. It is my belief that once we accept that we may not know how to do something or how to solve it that we are set free to explore and be open to what we find. My curiosity over the last two years has led me to study aspects of sociology, anthropology, psychology, communication, conversations and behavioural insights, together with the latest safety theory, just culture, resilience engineering, organisational safety and 'Safety II'. I have grown in my understanding about what safety really is. The culmination of that is this second book.

I mentioned in my first book that while preparing for a particular talk I was due to give I read Chris Anderson's book *TED Talks: The Official TED Guide to Public Speaking* (2016). He devoted a chapter to what was titled the throughline. He talked about how every talk needs to say something meaningful. He suggests applying a tool that is used in plays, movies and novels which is to use a throughline. This he says is the connecting theme that ties together each narrative element and that every talk should have one. Anderson suggested a good exercise, to try to encapsulate your throughline in no more than fifteen words. And those fifteen words need to focus people on the precise idea you want them to understand. I really liked this idea as a way of bringing to life my work, to construct a strong thread throughout all the elements of my book. A way of connecting everything together. In terms of this book – my 15-word throughline is:

> A balanced approach to safety addressing culture, conditions and values that help people work safely

This book aims to look beyond patient safety and to share my discovery of new approaches in order to push the margins about what we think about safety. It is for all of those people and everyone who is ready to change the way they view patient safety and change the way they do things to make the difference that everyone needs. I hope that *Implementing Patient Safety* offers you a practical guide to doing things differently. All I ask is that you are curious and show up with an open heart and mind.

Acknowledgements

Thank you to everyone I have shared this vision with; you helped hone my thinking and have given me the confidence to continue. I am hugely grateful for the people I have met along the way and the people who have influenced my thinking and provided me with their stories, tales of their messy reality together with articles, quotes, books to read and inspiration in spades.

Thanks to the artist James Munro for the hand-drawn illustrations within the book – you can find him at https://www.mistermunro.co.uk.

Thank you for the generosity of spirit and 'nailing it' all of the time with your knowledge and advice – not to mention the jokes – from the most wonderful collection of minds that are: Adrian Plunkett, Emma Plunkett, Chris Turner, Neil Spenceley, Pete Jeffries, Helen Hunt, Gemma Crossingham, Alison Jones and Alyson Walker.

Thank you to the most joyous group of people I have ever had the privilege to work with – the Sign up to Safety team – I cannot believe I got to work with people who I can truly say I love: Dane Wiig, Cat Harrison, Adam Mohamed, David Naylor, Sarah Garrett, Jane Reid, Catherine Ede, Owen Bennett, Anna Babic and Hannah Thompson. I am especially grateful to Sarah Garrett for taking the time to read the final draft and for providing her unique and wonderful insight and wisdom.

Finally, my love, adoration and thanks to Bradley Colmans, my husband, who has my heart forever and who always helps turn my rhetoric into something much more understandable. This book is all the richer for his contribution. My life would be nothing without him.

Author

Dr Suzette Woodward works in the English National Health Service (NHS). She is an internationally renowned expert in patient safety and has been studying safety in healthcare settings since the 1990s. Her particular areas of interest include implementation of patient safety and the translation of theory and public policy into practice. She has an exceptional ability to take complex issues and make them easy to understand as well as being able to weave together different threads in a unique and stimulating way.

Suzette is a trained general and paediatric nurse who specialised in paediatric intensive care nursing for over ten years. She has a Master's in Clinical Risk and a Doctorate in Patient Safety and was the recipient of the Ken Goulding Prize for Professional Excellence in 2008. Her research focused on implementation of national patient safety guidance. She is also a visiting professor for Imperial College University in London. Suzette was awarded the Daisy Ayris Medal for services to perioperative nursing in 2011, named one of the top 50 inspirational women in the NHS in 2013, one of the top 50 nurse leaders in the NHS in 2014 and one of the top clinical leaders in the NHS in 2014.

Her first book, *Rethinking Patient Safety*, and the accompanying blogs have helped shape the conversation on thinking differently about safety in healthcare and she is a sought-after speaker at international and national conferences, workshops, symposia and meetings, having delivered over 200 keynote addresses on patient safety.

Part One

Create a Balanced Approach to Safety

Healthcare is incredibly complex.

We need to LEARN from everything we do, all the time – when things GO RIGHT and when they don't.

1.1 Part One Introduction

Part One describes the growing sense of unease about the way we do safety in healthcare together with some exciting ways in which we can do it differently. It describes the dominant approach to patient safety in healthcare we use today. It will propose that while the dialogue about patient safety has increased significantly we have become stuck. Stuck in a world of bureaucracy, negativity and blame. The tone and methods of patient safety have led to disengagement especially of clinicians. All of the evidence so far necessarily calls into question the prevailing ways in which patient safety has been framed and addressed to date. An important challenge we all have now is how do we engage, motivate and mobilise people to work safely within this negative workplace and culture.

Thankfully, the way we think about safety is changing (Hollnagel 2013. Vincent and Amalberti 2016, Mannion and Braithwaite 2017). Part One, therefore, considers how we should shift our approach to safety from focusing purely on failure to studying how things happen on a daily basis, how they typically go right (Safety II), and how this needs to be balanced with the learning from failure (Safety I). I propose that there are a number of safety myths that are getting in the way of progress and I go on to share the latest thinking, the new models of safety and the ideas born out of complexity science and complex adaptive systems.

1.2 Failure

1.2.1 Negativity

In life we pay more attention to the negative things; the negative headlines in a newspaper, the negative reviews of an article we have written, the poor feedback about a talk we may have delivered. We all remember the negative comments in an appraisal rather than the positive comments. Even if there is a balance of positive and negative findings we put more weight on the negative ones and feel that the priority is to address the negative rather than the positive. Even if we get one negative comment and nine positive comments, we feel we have to change ourselves to meet that one comment rather than accept that most people liked it so there is no need to change. This in turn may mean that we change it so that only one person likes it and nine people don't. This attitude has 'infected' the world of safety. Consequently, negativity is considered more impactful that positivity. We constantly feel we have to change based on the negative things that happen rather than the positive.

This is the same in life as well as it is in safety. Pinker (2016) says that many people face the morning news with trepidation and dread. We are continually told that things are getting worse and that modern life is much more negative than our past. We pay attention to the stories of negativity and it leaves people longing for different times when it felt safer, kinder and more equitable. If we translate this to healthcare, what people do is pay attention to the bad news and pay attention to the stories which point to the feeling that the health service is getting worse. The media is particularly effective at pointing out where healthcare fails rather than where healthcare succeeds. And within healthcare safety we focus almost exclusively on the negative; what are the problems we need to address, what are the things we are doing that are going wrong, data collection systems, the number of incidents, accidents, never events, serious incidents, deaths, complaints and claims. The current methods used to study safety in healthcare are fixated on where we have failed in order to figure out how we can prevent those failures and improve the way we care for patients.

There is a desire to quantify the level of failure. Asking if healthcare is getting worse or better. Or whether it is less safe or safer. The following describes what the researchers and safety experts over the years have tried to do so far to find out the scale of the problem with the ultimate aim of being able to tell if we are getting safer or not.

1.2.2 Studies of Failure

Research in relation to failure can be tracked back to over a century and a half ago, since the time of Florence Nightingale and Ignaz Semmelweiss. Florence Nightingale wanted to study why some of her patients died and some didn't and what the causes of these differences were when she cared for the army in the Crimean War. This was from April 1854 to March 1855 and she believed that most of the illness (or harm) which afflicted the army was caused by defects in the system. She estimated that one in seven of her patients died from preventable diseases rather than their battle wounds and that the things that would reduce the 'harm' or illnesses included good nutrition, warm clothing, good ventilation, cleanliness and hygiene (Huxley 1975). The work of Ignaz Semmelweiss published in 1857 is often quoted as one of the first patient safety research studies into maternal morbidity and mortality and infection control. His work concluded that increased handwashing resulted in a reduction in mortality from infections for mothers and babies in his care. However, much of his findings were dismissed by his colleagues who refused to change their practice and Semmelweiss died well before his work would receive the recognition it deserved (Woodward 2017).

It is interesting to note that the contributory factors of both are similar to our knowledge today. The factors Nightingale found in relation to nutrition, clothing, ventilation, cleanliness and hygiene and the finding by Semmelweiss that washing hands made a significant difference to maternal morbidity and mortality have stood the test of time. So, there have been some clues and indicators for quite some time that we have yet to 'fix'.

Also in the late 1800s, another pioneer Ernest Codman took the radical step of publishing not only his patients' outcomes but also his judgements on whether the results could have been improved and the probable causes of failure to achieve 'perfection'. Codman graduated from Harvard Medical School in 1895 and interned at Massachusetts General Hospital. He joined the surgical staff of Massachusetts General and became a member of the Harvard faculty. While there, he introduced the first morbidity and mortality conferences. However, in a similar way to Semmelweiss, staff were nervous about his work and in 1914 the hospital refused his plan for evaluating the competence of surgeons and he lost his staff privileges there. Codman eventually established his own hospital (which he called the End Result Hospital) to pursue the performance measurement and improvement objectives he believed in so fervently. To support his 'end results theory' Codman made public the results of his own hospital; in which for the 337 patients discharged between 1911 and 1916, Codman recorded and published 123 errors (Woodward 2017).

1.2.3 Retrospective Case Note Reviews

Move forward over a hundred years and we find research studies which have tried to understand the scale and nature of the problem by auditing patient case notes. There are very few documented early studies of the subject but an example published in 1974 conducted in California studied patient records and estimated that out of three million hospital admissions there were 140,000 injuries, 24,000 being considered due to 'negligence' (Woodward 2017).

Since the late 1990s, the main method of study has therefore been to audit patient case notes which is usually described as 'retrospective case note review'. These case note review studies have been carried out across the world and have cited a range of incident rates ranging from 2.9% to 16.6% of all hospital admissions with preventable adverse event rates ranging from 1.0% to 8.6% (Woodward 2017). The first of these was undertaken in New York State (Brennan et al. 1991), the findings of which were extrapolated to suggest that as many as 98,000 patients in hospital settings in the US died each year as a result of problems related to their care. One of the following studies was undertaken in the UK in two acute hospitals by a team under the leadership of Vincent and colleagues (2001). This has led to the now often used 10% statistic in the UK (and possibly worldwide) which is used in a number of different ways such as 'on average there is a 10% error rate in healthcare' or simplified to things like '10% of patients in healthcare are harmed'.

Other examples include a study from New Zealand that concluded that 3.4% of 118 deaths were related to preventable errors in healthcare (Briant et al. 2006). A large retrospective case record review study of 21 of the 101 hospitals in the Netherlands reported a figure of 4.1% adverse events contributing to death among deceased patients (Zegers et al. 2009).

Hogan and a team of researchers conducted a retrospective case record review study in the UK in 2009 (Hogan et al. 2012). In this study of 1000 adults who died in 2009 in ten acute hospitals, reviewers judged 5.2% of deaths as having a 50% or greater chance of being preventable. Extrapolating from these figures the authors suggest there would have been 11,859 adult preventable deaths in hospitals in England in 2009. Hogan and her colleagues found that the problems associated with preventable deaths occurred in all phases of hospital care but were most likely in wards (44%) and involved poor clinical monitoring (31%), diagnostic errors (30%), or inadequate drug or fluid management (21%). Most preventable deaths (60%) occurred in elderly, frail patients with multiple comorbidities judged to have had less than one year of life left to live.

In a further study of deaths in England by Hogan and her colleagues the reviewers identified a preventable death rate of 3.6%, lower than the results in 2009 (5.2%), and no significant variation in the proportion of preventable deaths between hospitals (Hogan et al. 2016). This study was to determine the proportion of avoidable deaths in acute hospital trusts in England and to determine the association with the tools used to assess and compare hospitals on their mortality data; the hospital standardised mortality ratio (HSMR) and the summary hospital-level mortality indicator (SHMI). The reviewers studied 34 English acute hospital trusts (ten in 2009 and 24 in 2012/13) randomly selected from across the spectrum of HSMR. The difference between 2009 and 2015 is stated as:

■ In the 2012/13 cohort, the patients were sicker with a higher prevalence of several key comorbid conditions. Whether or not this was a real difference or reflected greater propensity to record these comorbidities, the impact on reviewers is likely to mean they were less likely to judge a death as avoidable.
■ Reviewers' awareness of the use of 'do not attempt resuscitation' orders was probably greater as a result of the wider use of highly visible forms in the case records plus changes to the medical review form, which drew their attention to such orders.
■ There was a minor difference in the wording of the question about attribution of avoidability.

There was a small but statistically non-significant association between HSMR and the proportion of avoidable deaths. The authors concluded that the small proportion of deaths judged to be avoidable meant that any metric based on mortality is *unlikely to reflect the quality of a hospital*. Therefore, the authors recommended that measuring mortality should be focused on identifying ways of improving the quality of care and not used as an indicator of safety in a hospital.

Assessing mortality using either retrospective record review or a hospital wide mortality ratio is not a helpful or informative indicator of the safety of a hospital. It is potentially misleading to the public, clinicians, managers, and commissioners to praise or condemn a trust on the basis of either measure.

Hogan 2015

1.2.4 Limitations in Measuring Safety

The measuring and monitoring of safety continues to be a challenge. As mentioned, retrospective case note review is a method based on experts' assessments of healthcare records, considering the quality and safety of care provided during an admission. Hogan and others have described the fallibility of even the most carefully structured case review (Lilford et al. 2010, Hogan 2016). Despite the provision of extensive training and support, experienced clinical reviewers often disagree on what constitutes an avoidable death and are influenced by a range of extraneous factors. Equally if used to assess whether a patient has been harmed it is highly subjective and requires significant experience in understanding the care being provided. It is also flawed as a methodology because patient case notes can never include every single thing that has happened to them. So the judgement is being made on incomplete data. The limitations and risks associated with retrospective case record review method include (Hogan 2016):

■ The poor reliability of the reviewers' judgements. This includes that the estimates of life expectancy are dependent on reviewers' judgement. Even using two reviewers has only moderate reliability, because of the subjective element in judgements of avoidability and the quality of care. There is often disagreement between reviewers.

∎ Outcome and hindsight bias influences the judgement of causation and preventability.
∎ Variations in the intensity of treatment delivered to the growing population of elderly, frail, multi-comorbid patients have the potential to impact on the number of errors and the small number of deaths occurring in each hospital will inevitably result in large random error around the measure.

While the estimated number of preventable hospital deaths may prove helpful in raising interest in patient safety and a commitment to improvement, overestimating the size of the problem and the risk to patients may induce unjustified levels of anxiety and fear among the public.

As Hogan states in her article, 'The Problem with Preventable Deaths' in the *BMJ Quality and Safety*, there are significant limitations to measuring mortality as a way to show improved safety as follows (Hogan 2016):

∎ None of the current approaches to measure safety truly take into account the complexity of healthcare and most are focused on in-hospital care rather than across the whole healthcare system from acute care through to the patients' home.
∎ Death is an uncommon outcome for many specialties including obstetrics, psychiatry and surgical specialties such as ophthalmology, so relatively small numbers of deaths means that random variation can have a large influence on trend data and it is unlikely to be an indicator of whether the specialty is safer or not.

- Nearly a quarter of all NHS hospital admissions are people aged over 75 years, and more than 40% of deaths occur in those older than 80 years; so half the UK population end their lives in hospital, with variation between hospitals depending upon the provision of end of life care, and preventability of death is often difficult to determine.
- The vast majority of deaths do not involve safety problems. Even when errors of commission or omission do occur, establishing the degree to which healthcare has contributed to death among very elderly, frail patients with serious illness and multiple comorbidities towards the end of their natural lifespan and with just days or hours to live is extremely difficult.

Hogan suggests an alternative approach (2016). She suggests that a review of the major causes of preventable healthcare-related harm could be used to estimate associated increased mortality e.g., deaths associated with venous thromboembolism, surgical complications or hospital-acquired infections or falls. She also suggests combining outcome with process measures to increase specificity when identifying preventable deaths, e.g., measuring pulmonary embolism in patients who die and who did not receive adequate venous thromboembolism measures.

In truth we don't really know the full extent of harm; we don't know the actual percentage of harm or things that 'go wrong' because it is impossible to measure.

In our current focus on 'the things that go wrong' if we wanted to know if we were getting any better we would need a definitive baseline in order to judge. However, we do not have this, we do not have a baseline of 'things that go wrong'. People don't know how many mistakes they could have made but for some reason didn't make them. They do not always recognise when they are about to get it wrong but then got it right. There are a also things that some people may consider are 'things that have gone wrong' but others think of as ways in which the system functions or are simply complications or side effects of the treatment. Thus, we will never be able to identify and capture all of the things that 'go wrong' or even agree if they are things that 'go wrong'.

We don't capture everything that goes wrong and we don't capture things that go right so we cannot have a percentage of things that go wrong over things that go right or vice versa. We don't have that because currently it is impossible to collect.

Added to this the fact that we don't measure the things that go right every single time because we have not found a way to measure something that seems invisible. This means that we do not truly understand the whole host of reasons and determinants as to why safety may have improved or not improved, why lives may have been saved or lost and why harm has been avoided or not and whether the measures cited in fact represent the truth or reality. While the measurement of safety seems somewhat impossible given the significant challenges discussed here, there is hope and progress in this area. I will share these later in the book.

1.3 Safety Myths

Despite efforts by many committed and well-intentioned policy makers, managers, clinicians, researchers and patient groups – improvements in safety have only been confined to a few notable examples (Mannion and Braithwaite 2017). Large areas of healthcare have been left behind with certain problems in healthcare safety; acute care, surgery, infections, getting more attention than others. Before I go any further in the book I think it is important to present a number of myths and misunderstandings in healthcare safety which need to be discussed and where possible addressed. This is because in themselves they are part of the problem, they are preventing the advances that we know could be made. With a nod back to the previous section, the first relates to the search for the scale and nature of the problem.

1.3.1 10% of Patients in Healthcare Are Harmed

One of the studies to quantify harm was undertaken in the UK in two acute hospitals by a team under the leadership of Vincent and colleagues (2001). As mentioned, this has led to the now often used 10% statistic in the UK (and possibly worldwide) which is used in a number of different ways such as 'on average there is a 10% error rate in healthcare' or simplified to things like '10% of patients in healthcare are harmed'. This statistic is used in the introduction of many policy documents, research studies, patient safety interventions, guidelines and so on and is often quoted in presentations and speeches on safety. While it is good to provide numbers as a 'call to action' or to galvanise people into action it is wrong to use a statistic that is not as factually accurate as they think.

The statistic has become a myth. In reality, the statistic was rounded up from a finding found in a retrospective case note review study. This study was undertaken in London (UK) and the researchers considered case notes from two acute hospitals. As discussed earlier the statistics are based on a flawed and subjective methodology. We therefore cannot say that on average there is a 10% error rate in healthcare. We can only say that based on a small research study in acute care within a town-based hospital care setting in the UK there is an indication that patients are harmed and that this may be around 10% of patients. Some of these harms may have been preventable and some of them not. I would suggest that people should stop using or promoting this number as the absolute i.e., the exact number related to unsafe care.

1.3.2 Incident Reporting Systems will Capture all the Things that Go Wrong

If retrospective case note reviews can only provide one aspect of the nature and scale of harm what about incident reporting systems? Actually, the same can be said for these systems. For many reasons incident reporting systems cannot capture everything that 'goes wrong in healthcare' even if there is some disagreement about the definition of what that is or what a patient safety incident is. Incident reporting systems capture different types of harm such as falls, pressure ulcers, undetected or late diagnosed sepsis, suicide, or medication errors. They capture the easy to report, and are mainly the reports submitted by one profession (nurses). Therefore, incident reports are merely indictors of what is happening in an organisation. They are brief triggers for further inquiry and can never be anything more than that (Macrae 2016). Safety professionals should help promote the fact that incident reporting will simply provide organisations and teams an indication of the way in which the system fails but does not describe the safety of the system.

1.3.3 Incident Reports Can Be Used to Prioritise Solutions and Activity

The reporting systems are used to prioritise resources and activity both at a national and local level. They therefore have a knock-on effect to prioritising action and activities that may not be as important to address as other issues that only have a handful of reports to their name. At a national level, the numbers and types of incidents reported are then used to shape patient safety policy, create patient safety alerts and other national interventions. This has the potential for the efforts and resources to be diverted to reported problems rather than the unknown or not reported.

The problem with incident reporting apart from the lack of learning is that it puts things in boxes. Organisations set up structures to tackle these harms, assign people with roles to concentrate on reducing the number of things in the box and an industry of short-term projects. Very rarely are these isolated harms looked at in combination or studied for the cross-cutting factors that thread through all of them.

The original intent of incident reporting systems was to identify the aspects in the system that were failing in some way, study these failures and reduce the chances of them happening again by putting in changes; barriers or new ways of working. To some extent they are a victim of their own success, if success is one of data collection. This path has led to the creation of an industry which feels far removed from the everyday workings of healthcare. For some reason the incidents have then been given different names in order to create somewhat false categories; incident reports, deaths, significant events, serious incidents, serious untoward events, adverse events, and never events. These terms are really all the same thing, the times when things went wrong or didn't go as planned. However, the implications for calling certain things serious incidents or never events is huge. Once they get labelled in this way those that scrutinise, oversee, regulate, or performance manage leap into action and bear down on an organisation or practice in a way that is intimidating and punitive.

1.3.4 Incident Reports and Investigations Provide Unambiguous Data (the Truth)

Investigations should be with the mindset that the information gained will never be all of the information. There is never 'one truth' but multiple truths. Additionally, we may not surface the truth because people are fearful of telling the truth. They are fearful of sharing the fact that they may not have followed policy or procedure or they may have done something wrong, so they tell the investigator what they want to hear.

The incident reports are a retrospective methodology filled with hindsight, outcome and confirmative bias and the information is of poor quality. All investigations are subject to the same bias and they are both reactive and retrospective. When something has gone wrong we inevitably have to look backwards and immediately start by finding the bits that make sense to us. Before the accident things don't look very clear but when we look back it appears clearer and then we make sense of the data in ways that may not have been the actual case.

The outcome is rarely clear before it happens. If the outcome is really bad then this influences how we see the behaviour that led up to it. Knowing the outcome of an event changes the way that the investigator thinks about the actions and decisions that took place in the run-up to that outcome. If you are involved in investigation, then your responsibility is to be mindful of your own biases, your own reaction to failure and the judgements and evaluations you make.

> Research has shown repeatedly that the exact same performance will be judged differently depending on the outcome.
>
> **Shorrock 2018c**

Outcome bias is confirmed in our everyday experience. Often, what makes our performance appear 'bad' is not the performance itself, but the outcome. In healthcare, this is particularly strong when someone has died. Had there been no accident, no incident or no death then the performance would often be judged as normal, even uneventful. In fact, as Shorrock says, perhaps they will even be seen as productive, efficient or effective.

Shorrock describes the misleading light of hindsight as a really strong bias. He defines it as the 'knew-it-all-along phenomenon' or 'creeping determinism', and refers to the common tendency for people to perceive events that have already occurred as having been more predictable than they actually were before the events took place. Hindsight plays a huge role in the way we handle the aftermath of an error, mistake or incident. With hindsight, it is easy to judge people for missing something that turned out to be critical and it is easy to see the harm that is assumed should have been foreseen and prevented.

Confirmation bias is the tendency to search for, interpret, favour and recall information in a way that confirms one's pre-existing beliefs or hypotheses. Knowledge of the incident can constrain the imagination. When investigating an incident it is really hard to ignore the knowledge of the actions taken, it is hard to disregard what did happen in order to focus on what should have happened.

1.3.5 We Should Aim for a Rise in Incident Reports Because It Demonstrates a Good Safety Culture

The incident reporting systems are a never-ending pursuit of rising reports. We count the number of failures and aim for a reduction in the failures while at the same time aim for an increase in the number of reports of failure. This has led to a huge industry and we are now drowning in data and one could ask at what point we stop. For example, the national reporting and learning system in the NHS in England has captured millions of reports since its inception in 2003. A large percentage of the data related to the 'easy to report' include falls and pressure ulcers. So, since 2003, there are millions of falls within this database. How much is enough?

If one were studying falls as part of a PhD one would want a large proportion of falls in order to identify the contributory and causal factors but would probably say any more than a thousand cases is enough let alone millions. Perhaps we need to stop collecting and shift our efforts to analysing what we already have.

> Incident reports are used as a threat – 'I will datix you'

Part of the reason why there are so many reports is that from the outset organisations were told that increased reports meant they had a good reporting culture which in turn meant they had a good safety culture. The mantra has led to organisations seeking an increase in numbers as the goal rather than the quality of reports and learning from those reports. This is perpetuated by external regulation and scrutiny. For example, the national system is used to rank hospitals in accordance with their reporting rates and this ranking is then used by regulators to decide on whether the organisation is good or not in terms of safety. In reality, incident reporting systems will never capture all the things that go wrong on a day-to-day basis and increased reporting may actually mean that there is a poor culture of learning.

> The pressure on organisations to increase reporting means that they capture reports just for the sake of increasing the numbers. These systems are being 'gamed' with people learning how to make their systems look like the reporting of incidents is healthy. Everyone aims to be in the middle of any league table, it is the place of least interest to those that scrutinise reporting behaviours. What we have created is a culture of mediocrity.

1.3.6 A Reduction in Incident Reports Means We Are Learning

Does a reduction in incident reports mean we are learning? Actually, reduced reports of a particular type might simply indicate that people are becoming accustomed to something happening, or have grown tired of reporting or stopped noticing the problem in question. Thus, when reports decline, incident data on their own cannot distinguish between a reassuring improvement in safety or a concerning organisational blind spot (Macrae 2016).

The focus on the quantity of incidents reported rather than the quality of information has perpetuated a range of interrelated problems. Instead of developing as a critical way in which an organisation or a team can learn about what is going on in their area of healthcare they have become simply a counting machine. The original ambitions have been forgotten and now all people do is collect the problems. There is little time to investigate and address the problems or to share the resulting lessons.

Safety professionals should apply current and more up to date methods for looking at the whole system – when it functions well and when it doesn't. Even within incident reporting systems there is a need for more sophisticated ways to learn from incident reports and incident investigations and we need to redesign healthcare incident reporting systems so that they achieve the following principles (Macrae 2016):

- Redesign your reporting strategy so that it avoids swamping the reporting system.
- Learn about serious, specific or surprising insights into the system and use the reports to identify and prioritise significant or new risks.
- Expect reports to be inaccurate and incomplete – the subsequent investigation should be used to obtain the complete picture.

■ Do not use them as performance management or a measure of safety or a measure of a safety culture.
■ Free up time focused on capturing failure so that people can focus on success.

1.3.7 Incident Investigations and Root Cause Analysis Will Identify the Causes of What Happened

In the last two decades, healthcare has tried to adopt models used in other high-risk industries, especially that of aviation, in order to explain why incidents happen. The predominant method has been root cause analysis, and other similar cause and effect ideologies. There is an assumption that investigations will enable us to find out why things happened and we will be able to identify the root cause of the problem and fix it.

In the UK health system, organisations are expected to investigate multiple incidents within a framework which puts a cap on the time in which an investigation can be carried out (60 days). However, time is not the only pressure to find 'the' cause. There is pressure, rightly, from the patient and their family and from the staff involved. But there is also pressure from internal and external people; those that lead, those who commission and those who provide oversight and scrutiny. Assigning causes to an incident makes us happy because it means we have an explanation, in particular, an explanation we can share with those that scrutinise or who are anxious for the answers but there are many instances when the cause may never be found. However, very few people can accept that in many instances things 'just happen' and when a cause has not been found it calls into doubt the credibility of the investigator or investigation.

As humans, we like to find neat answers. There is a belief that when something goes wrong there must be 'a' cause and we assume we will find the preceding cause. Everyone likes a cause, even better if it is a single cause. This means that the investigators may latch on to a superficial cause to the exclusion of more fundamental causes. For example, if they found that people didn't follow a policy or communicate well or didn't perform a task well then the recommendation is to 'tell people to follow the policy', provide 'communication training' and 'retrain staff' in relation to tasks. The search for information is stopped when an acceptable explanation has been found even though this may be incomplete or incorrect. Most of the time investigations find shallow contributory factors rather than deep root causes and while addressing these contributory factors may help it will not prevent things from going wrong in the future. A report with a list of recommendations, the more the better, whether implementable or not enables people to shut down any further need for more study. So, the search for a root cause is a fallacy, another myth and this search is preventing us from working on what matters and we end up by working on something that is falsely labelled 'the cause'.

Interestingly, the things we assign causes to are things that are going on all of the time and sometimes they go right and sometimes they go wrong. In fact, there are very few things that can be deemed a preventable root cause, and very few things that can be addressed so that things will never happen again in the future. This is because, as we shall see later on in the book, systems are complex and adapt all of the time, outcomes emerge as a result of a complex network of contributory interactions and decisions and not as a result of a single causal factor or two. Incidents are disordered and there is no such thing as find, analyse and fix.

It is important to note also that given the adaptive nature of complex systems, the system after an incident is not the same as the system before it, many things will have changed, not only as a result of the outcome but as a result of the passing of time (Shorrock 2017). So, when it comes to incident investigations healthcare is challenging to understand (let alone measure, optimise and improve) because the investigator has to truly understand the variabilities and dynamics of the system and the often vague or shifting performance. There is always going to be a gap between how we think incidents happen and how they actually happen. In a complex system, you cannot assume that because two events occur together or one after the other that there is a correlation or causal relationship between those two events. By claiming one event must have caused the other there is a danger that a wrong conclusion could be made or even another unlooked for event may be missed. You cannot assume that there is only one explanation for the observation that is being made when in fact there will be undoubtedly many different explanations. In general, work evolves over time, and prescribed work proves too inflexible or too fragile to cope with real conditions. Over the longer term, these adaptations may result in a drift from prescribed policy, procedure, standard or guideline, assuming any such prescription is in place (Shorrock 2017).

Causality gets confused with correlation. For example, the correlation between solutions and causes. If the number of incident reports reduces, then there is the danger of an assumption that the solutions that were put in place as a result of the incident investigation resulted in increased safety whereas there could and probably is a multiple number of variables that need to be considered. To truly understand the effects it comes back to the common denominator and understanding what that is for aspects of safety. However, as I and others argue we do not have common denominators for safety.

We also believe that there is a positive or negative value associated with the cause. If the outcome was bad or a failure then the cause must have been bad or a failure. If the outcome was good then the cause must have been good. This symmetry makes us feel as if there is an order in the system.

Hollnagel 2016

1.3.8 Linear Cause and Effect Models Will Work in Healthcare

There are theoretical and practical consequences of root cause analysis on day-to-day operations, strategic management and planning, safety culture and organisational safety (Hollnagel 2013). Hollnagel's view is that simple linear accident models were appropriate for the work environments of the 1920s (when they were first conceived) but not for the current work environments. Even Professor James Reason the 'inventor' of the Swiss cheese model of investigation and accident causation argues that they have their limitations. The criticism of this model being that it does not account for the detailed interrelationships among causal factors and that the model while is useful to help think about the complexity of failure it does not explain where the holes are, what they consist of, why they are there in the first place and why they change over time or even how the holes get lined up to produce an accident (Eurocontrol 2006). In fact, it is interesting to note that Reason's definition of a root cause as 'the contributory factor that you are working on when the money or the time runs out'.

Accidents and incidents come in many sizes, shapes and forms and it is, therefore, naïve to hope that one model or one type of explanation will be universally applicable. Some incidents are really simple and some are really complex so different models are required. These models and methods require that systems are linear with resultant outcomes. In fact, healthcare is far from a linear system, where outcomes are emergent rather than resultant. The typical features of a complex healthcare system are random acts, changing context and conditions. Complexity models attempt to move us away from the naivety of conventional linear or straight line thinking and causality i.e., 'if we do x it will inevitably result in Y' or 'z happened because of x followed by y followed'. I will explore this in more detail in the section titled Complexity.

There are many times when I have investigated an incident and the cause has been elusive. Even with something as significant as administering the wrong drug to the wrong patient it was hard to truly understand why that happened. This is because while the outcome is clear the same is not the case for the actions that led to the outcome. In healthcare, in particular, the actions are likely to be due to transient conditions, literally things present in one time only at that particular place. Those same set of conditions may not actually happen ever again. This means that we cannot fix them in the same way as you would a linear process or technical fault. We may not be able to control every condition that happens. The only thing we can do is to minimise the error producing conditions in some way.

1.3.9 We Simply Need to Learn from Aviation (Or Other High Risk Industries)

Over the last few years, there has been a desire to learn from other high-risk industries. It is quite right to seek knowledge from other industries that appear to have improved the safety of their operations. There are undoubtedly things we can learn, for example, the use of checklists and team work as well as the way in which human factors science is embedded into the everyday fabric of these industries.

However, we need to reject the idea that all healthcare needs to do is learn from aviation (Vincent and Amalberti 2016). As Catchpole said on Twitter (12 December 2019),

> aviation boils down to solvable Newtonian physics, with engineering a central mediator. Healthcare is an unsolvable set of human existence problems, where tech is not a primary mediator. Safety engineering looks very different in both, so we need to translate, not transplant. And as Erik Hollnagel said in an interview in 2019, If every patient was as standard as an airplane it would be easy [to make care safer].

Perhaps instead of being like the aviation industry, we should aim to be like the sports industry. In sport, individuals study how they get it right and how others get it right in order to influence their technique; in order to get better at baseball or cricket or tennis they study how others do it well and how good their own performance is in order to optimise and improve it.

1.4 Concepts and Theories

Along with attempts to understand how healthcare fails and how safety in healthcare has been measured so far there have also been advances over the last one hundred years or so in respect of the concepts and theories associated with safety and healthcare. The most recent of these have been developed by experts including Reason, Vincent and Amalberti together with the resilience engineers and patient safety experts including Hollnagel, Braithwaite, and Wears, Leape, Plsek, Greenhalgh, Berwick and more. These are the people who have been at the forefront of creating a balanced approach to safety.

I will touch on a few of these within the book as a way to highlight their impact on thinking today. If as you read you want much more detail I would urge you to read the work of Reason and Vincent in particular. Reason developed the 'Swiss cheese model' and the theories associated with organisational conditions that produced error. He believed that accidents were caused by both active (frontline errors and mistakes) and latent conditions (decisions made at the design stage or by 'managers'). Reason is still considered one of the world's leading thinkers on safety and much of his work still resonates today. His work quite simply shifted many people's thinking away from seeing safety as either the problem of the system or the problem of the human but the interaction between the two. His work has in many respects been at the forefront of moving away from the blame culture to one that is just and fair and created that balanced approach that we are all still seeking.

Vincent helped develop our thinking around risk and risk management and has been at the forefront of incident investigation and the measurement and monitoring of safety. His work with Amalberti (2016) on strategies for safer healthcare is a must-read for anyone working in healthcare. Their beautifully articulated book *Safer Healthcare* (2016) helpfully defines different components of the health care system from ultra-safe to high–reliability to ultra-adaptive. All of which are relevant and needed in healthcare as they apply to the different clinical contexts within which care is provided. This is not about choosing one of these models and making it fit to all of healthcare but much more about identifying which of the system is which and applying the relevant safety strategies and interventions for managing and improving patient safety across these very different aspects of healthcare.

Three areas I will delve in more detail in the next few sections are that of implementation science, the three models of safety, complex adaptive systems and the combination of 'Safety I' and 'Safety II'.

1.5 The Three Models of Safety

There is a recognition that strategies for managing safety in highly standardised and controlled environments such as radiotherapy are necessarily different from those in which clinicians and others constantly have to adapt and respond to the changing circumstances they are faced with such as the emergency department of a general practice in the community. Because of this variability Vincent and Amalberti (2016) provide really helpful suggestions in relation to the variety of safety strategies and interventions.

1.5.1 Summary of the Three Models of Safety

The three models summarised by Vincent and Amalberti (2006) are:

1. Ultra adaptive – Embracing risk – Taking risks is the essence of the profession. The model required is that of experts who rely on personal resilience, personal expertise and technology to survive and prosper in the adverse conditions.
2. High reliability – Managing risk – Risk is not sought out but is inherent in the profession. The model required is that of the devolved groups who can organise themselves, provide mutual support, and who are allowed to adapt and make sense of their environment.
3. Ultra safe – Avoiding risk – Risk is excluded as far as possible. The model lends itself to regulation and supervision of the system to avoid exposing frontline staff and patients to unnecessary risk.

The authors' view is that we need to distinguish the three models approve to the management of risk, each with its own characteristic approach. Each one gives rise to a way of organising safety with its own characteristic approach and its own possibilities of improvement (Vincent and Amalberti 2016). The authors also provide a new and broader vision for addressing patient safety that encompasses care throughout the patient's journey including care at home. It helps us also study how safety is managed in different contexts and to develop a wider strategic and practical vision in which patient safety is recast.

1.5.2 The Three Models in Relation to Healthcare

- Examples of an ultra-adaptive environment are emergency medicine or community general practice (GPs). These are areas that have a very high level of autonomy. Becoming safer is about helping people adapt and respond to the difficult situations they face. It is also about recognising that emergency medicine and other ultra-adaptive environments will never be free from harm. These are the areas where prescribing care is very hard to do and people need to be trusted to constantly adapt and adjust what they do.

- Examples of a high–reliability system are scheduled surgery, obstetrics and midwifery. These areas are reliant on personal skill and resilience but in a more prepared and disciplined way. The risks while not entirely predictable are known and understood. In these areas, risk management is a constant concern. Just to note that high–reliability organisations as a concept have been considered for a few years now with organisations aiming to detect and respond to risk more proactively. These are the areas that need some prescribing but also need to be able to adapt when needed. For example, the induction of anaesthesia in the operating room needs to follow a clear sequence of activities and decisions reliably every time.

- Examples of an ultra-safe system are blood transfusion, microbiology, and radiotherapy. These areas are reliant on standardisation, automation and the avoidance of risk wherever possible. The skills required in these areas are knowledge and execution of standard operating procedures and practised routines. This approach also relies on external oversight, rules and regulation. These are the areas that lend themselves to prescribing care and do require as much detail as possible to be written down. For example, the delivery of chemotherapy requires a high degree of accuracy in terms of the amount prescribed and a clear adherence to rules around prescribing and administration.

However, like all things, there is no such thing as a one size model for patients who are subjected to all three of these models, sometimes within the same healthcare 'admission'.

For example, a patient who is in a road traffic accident will be treated by paramedics and the ambulance service who will need to respond in an ultra-adaptive way. The patient will need to be assessed, diagnosed and treated in accordance with not only what has happened to them but where it has happened. The patient will then be transported to the emergency department who will also need to react to the patient's condition which will change over time. The patient may require surgery and then they get to experience the ultra-adaptive system of anaesthesiology and surgery together with post-operative recovery and ward care. During their time in hospital, they may be given a blood transfusion and will undoubtedly be tested and if necessary treated for infection and electrolyte imbalance which require an ultra-safe system. The patient may have needed resuscitation and defibrillation which also require an ultra-safe system of administration in terms of the right amount of medication and administration of shock.

Underpinning these models is the system migration concepts by Amalberti. His work on system migration is an extremely influential model for safety and helps us understand, in particular, violations. Violations are described as times when people don't follow the rules and standards – deviations from the instructions. There are many reasons why violations happen and Amalberti describes the gradual shift to the 'boundary of safety' which combines a dynamic systems view of safety and risk with the psychological appreciation of the behavioural drivers underlying violations (Vincent et al. 2013).

Amalberti describes how deviations from instructions may become normalised and how we can go from working safely to taking more risks and then going even further. An example often used is driving. We all know in the UK we are supposed to drive on motorways (freeways) at a maximum speed of 70 miles per hour, but occasionally people shift into a risky speed of around 70 to 75 (described as 'illegal normal') but then even more rarely people may increase their risky behaviour by driving at around 80 miles per hour, and in some very minor occurrences some people may go much higher than this (illegal-illegal). We shift our behaviour because of demand, external pressures, individual and social forces. In healthcare, Amalberti suggests it is likely to be between less than 1% and 5% of people who take extreme risks, or are reckless in their behaviour.

1.6 Complex Adaptive Systems

Despite, as Erik Hollnagel says, complexity being a monolithic concept it is worth digging a bit deeper about what it means and why it might be worth considering when we look to helping people work safely.

1.6.1 Complexity Science

Complexity science can be used to understand the dynamic nature of the system, the relationships, the way that care is delivered and its interactional characteristics. Superficial conceptualisations of safety systems will not do. We need to form a more in-depth knowledge of the nature of the healthcare complex adaptive system and its resilience (Mannion and Braithwaite 2017). By understanding this can we then think about narrowing the gap between what people do and what people imagine they do.

Complexity science has evolved in part from systems theory and aims to help us understand what constitutes the complex system (and complex adaptive system) and to identify the common characteristics. Complexity means that a system has many variables which are continuously changing and 'dynamic complexity' refers to situations where cause and effect are subtle and where the effects over time of interventions are not obvious. Complexity scientists aim to study the properties and characteristics of the entire system; the dynamics, the independent and interdependent relationships that make up the system, and the emergent behaviours of the system. Therefore, complexity science is considered an increasingly useful conceptual framework for understanding how healthcare is delivered, how people within it can be supported and how it can be optimised.

1.6.2 Simple, Complicated and Complex

Glouberman and Zimmerman (2002) neatly describe the difference between simple, complicated and complex.

Following a cake recipe is simple. There are clear instructions on what you need in order to make the cake down to the tiniest measurements and this is backed up with detailed step by step guidelines for using the ingredients. The process for making the cake is usually standardised and has been tried and tested many times so that the best way to make the particular cake is there for all to use. Success comes from following the recipe. There are some variables; skill, scales, equipment such as ovens, the size and shape of the baking tins and so on but in the main, if you follow the recipe you should get a cake at the end of it.

Sending a rocket to the moon is complicated. It sounds complex, but complexity scientists consider it to be complicated because it can be broken down into a series of 'simple' problems and tasks. There are clearly factors that can lead to success or failure, it takes lots of different people, teams and a high level of expertise, plus lots of rules and regulations. But similar to our cake recipe there is a likelihood that the rocket is similar to ones before it and there is so much studied and tested about the rocket that every attempt to rule out uncertainty is done. Similar again to the cake making, the task also gets more certain over time – the more rockets sent to the moon the more assurance there is that the next one will be ok. Once you learn how to send a rocket to the moon you can repeat the process and perfect it. There is a degree of certainty about both what you are doing and of the outcome.

Raising a child is complex. Each child is unique and so raising one child will give you some experience but no assurance of success with the next one. Expertise can help but there is no certainty of success or failure. Each child may require an entirely different approach from the previous one. There is huge uncertainty about the outcome and it is dependent on a massive amount of variables. However, we do know it is possible to raise a child even if it is considered complex.

Knowing the difference between the three is important because they all require different skills, different resources and responses. Too often we try to simplify a complex problem and seek the simple solution. We try to implement solutions that are inappropriate for the degree of complexity.

> It is clear that healthcare is a complex adaptive system but within it, there are some processes that are simply complicated and in some instances just simple.

In healthcare (even though as you will see a little later it is classified as a complex adaptive system) there is a mix of simple, complicated and complex processes.

Intubating a patient is simple. Without wishing to upset my anaesthetic friends it could be possibly described as simple. There are clear instructions on what you need in order to intubate patients down to the tiniest measurements of medication and this is backed up with detailed step by step guide for using the medications and equipment. The process is usually standardised as per the size and weight and age of the patient and has been tried and tested many times so that the best way to intubate is there for all to use. Success comes from following the guidance or standard operating procedure. There are some variables; skill, patient factors, equipment, the size and shape of the airway and so on but in the main, if you follow the guidance you should be able to intubate a patient.

Routine surgery is complicated. Again like sending a rocket to the moon, it sounds complex, but one could consider it to be complicated because routine (and that is the crucial word) surgery can be broken down into a series of 'simple' problems and tasks. There are clearly factors that can lead to success or failure, it takes lots of different people, teams and a high level of expertise. But a routine surgery such as a tonsillectomy or a knee or a hip replacement is similar to ones before it and there is so much studied and tested about these types of surgery that every attempt to rule out uncertainty is done. The more the surgery is carried out the more certain it becomes over time – the more hips replaced the more assurance there is that the next one will be ok. Once you learn how to take tonsils out, replace knees or hips you can repeat the process and perfect it. There is a degree of certainty about both what you are doing and of the outcome.

Emergency care is complex, non-routine surgery, patients with rare diseases and multiple comorbidities, running a hospital or providing GPs are all complex. Each patient is unique and so caring for one patient will give you some experience but no assurance of success with all the others. Expertise can help but there is no certainty of success or failure. Each patient may require an entirely different approach from the previous one. There is huge uncertainty about the outcome and it is dependent on a massive amount of variables.

1.6.3 Healthcare

I have spoken to many safety experts from other high-risk industries and without fail they say that healthcare is more complex than any other industry, from nuclear power to aviation. The study of healthcare as a complex adaptive system has been considered for at least two decades (Plsek and Greenhalgh 2001, Glouberman and Zimmerman 2002). Plsek and Greenhalgh wrote in 2001:

■ The science of complex adaptive systems provides important concepts and tools for responding to the challenges of health care in the 21st century.
■ Clinical practice, organisation, information management, research, education, and professional development are interdependent and built around multiple self-adjusting and interacting systems.
■ In complex systems, unpredictability and paradox are ever present, and some things will remain unknowable.
■ New conceptual frameworks that incorporate a dynamic, emergent, creative, and intuitive view of the world must replace traditional 'reduce and resolve' approaches to clinical care and service organisation.

Common characteristics of complex adaptive systems are that of emergence and non-linear dynamics; the systems can move from, or include different areas of stability to very unstable behaviour. This is why as mentioned previously, retrospective root cause analysis is so difficult. Characteristics of complex adaptive systems include:

■ Relationships are key.
■ There are multiple components and interactions between people and components are dynamic and frequently unpredictable.

- The systems are flexible and do not lend themselves to standardisation as the interactions are non-linear and new patterns emerge and evolve all of the time.
- The people are constantly adaptive.

There is a view that a complex adaptive system requires local ownership and self-direction, allowing the people within it to have a freedom to act in relation to their own problems. It is too complex to be operated by central command and control and needs to be organised from the bottom up. If healthcare is made up of multiple groups of people, professions and specialisms across vastly different care settings how do we build on current structures and relationships that help people adjust and adapt what they do safely to enhance the healthcare system?

Structures that work well in complex adaptive systems, therefore, include self-organisation, distributed leadership and devolved decision making which are rare in today's healthcare. Healthcare would benefit from distributed leadership that trusts people and values them and their skills rather than the position they sit in. Each person should be given a part to play in terms of leading on aspects of the system and they must be given permission to make decisions based on their expertise and experience and not have to ask the 'leader at the top'. There is always a need to have one person who can take responsibility when needed and to nurture the team around them but they are not to be seen as the ones who have all the answers or expected to be the ones making all the decisions.

Complexity science forces us to consider the dynamic and non-dynamic properties of healthcare and the varying characteristics, forces, variables and influences across it. This includes understanding the flow across and within different sections of the system from GPs, to ambulance services and emergency departments and beyond. These need to allow people to operate successfully within a constantly changing and unpredictable environment. Complexity science recognises that some areas of healthcare are predictable and certain, while some areas are 'normally' unpredictable and uncertain as we saw earlier with the 'three models of safety' (Vincent and Amalberti 2016). Healthcare attempts to function effectively with all these differing actors and respond by providing care and clinical treatment that is tailored for specific patient needs.

If we want to change or improve or strengthen a complex system like healthcare we need to look for patterns in the behaviour of the system. We need to look for interconnections within the system rather than isolated problems. In safety, this means looking at the things that occur in relation to lots of incidents and not simply the incidents in isolation. Importantly, we need to be careful when attributing cause and effect in a complex adaptive system, as we have seen it is very rarely that simple. Equally we should be careful about prediction. Prediction can never be certain – things happen when you least expect them to in healthcare. Therefore, keep in mind that the system is dynamic, and it doesn't necessarily respond to intended change as predicted.

Healthcare is changing all of the time and cannot be pulled apart in the same way. Its behaviour is also momentary so even if there is an attempt to understand it at one time or one point it will have changed before that understanding has been explained. We owe it to people who work in the frontline of healthcare to better understand how to work in a complex adaptive system.

A complex adaptive system can be quite different from how we imagine it. This is why we need to truly understand work-as-done. In that respect, there are different approaches required. A complicated system can be described in detail and pulled apart to consider how it is designed, what the steps are and how they can be improved, perhaps one by one. It can be linear with a simple causality approach and complicated systems can assume predictability and be measured. For example, the traditional approach used in quality improvement and lean methodology fits for a complicated system. For example, quality improvement attempts to break down the whole system or task and work out why it failed or why it succeeded in some areas and failed in others. Which is why in healthcare some of the improvement projects work for simple and complicated aspects of healthcare but don't work well for complex areas. Solutions have to be matched, simple solutions for simple areas and problems, complicated solutions for complicated problems and complex solutions for complex systems.

> Quality improvement, analytical and investigatory methods are more appropriate for complicated tasks than complex systems because they rely on a linear process or a process pipeline that flows from one step to another until the process reaches an end point.

Top-down interventions that are designed for complicated systems and imposed on complex ones will not make a difference to the everyday reality. This is in part why it is so difficult to engage some staff in quality improvement projects or to disengage them when the projects do not seem to work. In this respect, it is also really hard to convert policy into action. A complex system rarely responds to full-scale change preferring incremental rather than transformative approaches. Designing a flow chart, that would work beautifully for a complicated task, would for a complex problem only end in frustration.

1.6.4 Complexity and Dilemmas

Healthcare is full of dilemmas, of choices or decisions between two or more alternatives and often between two things that are equally undesirable. A dilemma is defined as a situation in which a difficult choice has to be made between two or more alternatives, especially ones that are equally undesirable. There are many different words people use for a dilemma; difficult decision, catch-22, quandary, predicament, puzzle, conundrum or awkward situation. Dilemmas are created when there are competing goals and trade-offs between productivity and safety, flow and safety, efficiency and thoroughness, compete versus collaborate; reduce costs versus keep people safe; keep all patients safe versus keeping one patient safe.

Like all high-risk industries, work in healthcare is rarely about certainty and predictability. There are a huge number of stakeholders with conflicting goals, multifaceted interactions and constraints, and multiple perspectives which change daily. The choices and decisions people make in healthcare can often have no right or wrong answer.

A dilemma can be as a result of the divergent needs that policy makers, managers, clinicians and others have and the choices they have to make to meet those differing needs. There can be opposing forces and strong views on either side of the dilemma. This results in clinical staff and managerial staff being faced with having to choose between adhering to one policy and another with conflicted requirements. Ultimately, there is a pressure to force someone to choose either of the two unfavourable alternatives. Let us consider two examples; one local the other global.

1.6.4.1 A Local Dilemma

In the National Health Service (NHS), governments have set targets over the years such as guaranteeing maximum waiting times for non-emergency surgery or guaranteeing a maximum four-hour wait in the emergency department. These targets have been blamed for distorting clinical priorities and with limited resources decisions can cause conflicts especially when one target is challenged by another. For example, ambulances have been forced to queue up outside busy emergency departments which means that the ambulances might not be able to meet their target in responding to emergency calls, but the hospital can meet its four-hour emergency department target.

The four-hour target is the need to assess and either admit patients from the emergency department within four hours or send them home. This target can mean that a clinician has to make a difficult choice. Take, for example, a patient who has a suspected heart problem. If there was no target the emergency department staff may just keep the patient for a few hours to monitor them. However, because of the target they have to move them somewhere; admit them into the hospital or send them home. This is the first dilemma, the pressure to discharge patients that they would rather keep an eye on but don't want to admit or the pressure to admit patients that don't need to be admitted because they don't want to send them home yet. The second dilemma in this example comes when the choice of bed is limited. For example, there may be no beds on the cardiac ward. The choice is, therefore, to breach the four-hour target while waiting for a bed on the cardiac ward or to send them home or to place them on another ward that does not specialise in heart problems. This means that the patients may be admitted to areas that have a bed rather than the area where they will be treated by people who are expert in their particular problem.

The senior sister on a cardiac ward knows that to keep her patients safe, they should be sent from the emergency department to her ward. She also knows that her hospital is judged by its compliance with the four-hour wait in the emergency department. She knows that patients tend to be safer out of the emergency department and the individual patient admitted to a different ward, such as an orthopaedic ward, may be at greater risk because staff are unfamiliar with their condition.

1.6.4.2 A Global Dilemma

Antimicrobial resistance is the ability of a microbe to resist the effects of medication (antibiotics) that once could successfully treat the microbe. Resistant bacteria are more difficult to treat, requiring alternative medications or higher doses. Microbes resistant to multiple antimicrobials are called multidrug resistant. Antimicrobial resistance is increasing globally because of greater access to and prescription of antibiotic drugs. Preventive measures include only using antibiotics when needed, thereby stopping misuse of antibiotics or antimicrobials. This dilemma has led to the development of programmes for antibiotic stewardship aimed at persuading doctors to refrain from prescribing antibiotics in marginal cases.

A particular dilemma in relation to antibiotic use is that of patients with sepsis. Sepsis is a life-threatening condition that arises when the body's response to infection causes injury to its own tissues and organs. Sepsis is usually treated with the giving of intravenous fluids and antibiotics as soon as possible, usually within one hour of potential diagnosis. However, some severe infections such as sepsis are often deceptively trivial. The dilemma is; does the clinicians hold off on the prescribing of antibiotics or prescribe the antibiotics 'just in case'. But if sepsis is missed this could result in significant harm or even the death of a patient if they do not receive their antibiotics quickly. So this is a very real pressure. There is also the 'threat' associated with not prescribing antibiotics because there have been a number of cases of untreated sepsis and patients dying as a result in the UK which have led to staff being judged as making the wrong decision and being punished or castigated for not prescribing or administering the antibiotics. But it is never that simple. The pressure not to give and the pressure to give is a really difficult dilemma in healthcare today. It can have the knock-on effect of treating patients inappropriately or not treating them enough.

No intensive care beds. The ability to admit and operate on a routine or an emergency patient versus moving sick
patients from intensive care to a ward earlier than normal so
that the patient can be cared for postoperatively.

- A patient is on the waiting list as routine or an emergency
  patient is admitted for neurosurgery.
- Neurosurgical patients generally require a period of time
  in intensive care.
- The intensive care unit is full. However, there are some
  patients who are on the verge of being transferred to the
  ward.
- The clinicians would prefer the intensive care patient
  to remain for observation for a bit longer. The surgeons
  would like to operate on their patient quickly. The managers want to ensure that the waiting lists are reduced
  and that patients are seen as soon as they need to be.
  The surgical patients would like to have their operation
  quickly. The intensive care patients would like to stay in
  intensive care a bit longer.
- The ward nurses and doctors are nervous about receiving an intensive care patient too early. There may not
  be enough nurses or doctors to care for a patient that
  requires possible high-dependency care.
- There is the possibility that the intensive care patient
  will deteriorate when on the ward and need to return to
  intensive care.
- And so again... everyone wants the best for the patients
  but they have different incentives and pressures. The different purposes causes tension and conflict.

Send a patient home from the GPs clinic. Being a general
practitioner is extraordinarily hard. They are presented with a
patient who may or may not be able to articulate their signs
and symptoms and how they are feeling and based on a small
amount of information gained in a very short time the GP has

to decide in relation to a patient who may have a condition that is serious and will get worse or a condition that will get better or no condition at all.

- The patient is referred immediately to hospital. The patient will go to hospital and add to the workload of that hospital and be found not to have a serious condition so the decision was the wrong one. Or they do have something serious and will need the care the hospital can provide so the decision was the right one.
- The patient is sent home and asked to come back immediately or to go to hospital immediately if they get worse. The patient goes home and gets worse but fails to return to the GP or go to hospital (either they did not understand the urgency or the information or they were frightened). The decision is the wrong one. Or they go home but come back when they feel worse and the illness becomes clearer so the decision is the right one. Or they go home and get better and the decision was the right one.
- The patient is sent home and referred for specialist outpatient review. The patient goes on the waiting list, gets an outpatient appointment and they are successfully treated and the decision was the right one. Or the patient goes on the waiting list, gets an outpatient appointment and there is nothing wrong with them. The decision (while it assured the patient that there was nothing wrong) may still be the wrong one.

1.6.4.3 Let's Talk about It

The first step in addressing dilemmas is to talk about dilemmas. It is vital that the different stakeholders talk together about the mutually exclusive propositions that people face. If we talk about dilemmas and the challenges that arise for leadership and frontline staff we may find a way to expose them and reveal the hidden trade-offs or adjustments that are kept secret because people are fearful of the consequences. How can we make the right decision? This is what a complex adaptive system is all about. In all these there are questions to ask such as:

- Which one has more risk than the other?
- Which one will benefit more than the other?
- Based on experience and expertise which is the more likely outcome?

For example, in the case of the four-hour target the different stakeholders actually have similar goals of efficiency, effectiveness and safety. The government set a target of four-hours wait in the emergency department because they don't want the public to be waiting unnecessarily before they get treatment, they think this will incentivise organisations to make their departments more efficient. Clinicians want their patients to be safe and also don't want their patients to wait longer than necessary. The managers within the organisation are measured on this target and are therefore keen for no patients to wait longer than four hours and they also feel it is the right thing to do, they too want the patients to be safe. Everyone wants the best for the patients but they have different incentives and pressures and these differences cause tension and conflict. So the way of addressing the dilemma is to work out what those similar goals are and how each of these goals can be met in some way. It is never down to one person or one team. Therefore, the senior sister is helped by exposing what is actually going on (work-as-done) and by a shared responsibility for the dilemma.

Articulating dilemmas helps to make explicit how people are expected to manage them. It helps us to find a way forward which is not simply about giving more weight to one side of the dilemma than the other. By talking about dilemmas it could help us get closer to what is being ignored that may be relevant to safety and how this ignoring is woven into the very fabric of the way an organisation frames what is going on. We know we need to find a way of creating a shared conversation; one that brings people with competing interests and incentives into a conversation that sees keeping people safer as means of doing the right thing, saving money and meeting the targets.

1.7 Safety I and Safety II

In this section, I want to focus on the emerging view about safety that has been developed over the last six years primarily from the thinking of leading experts in healthcare, patient safety and resilience engineering and the connection between all three. This thinking builds on all of the concepts and theories discussed in the previous sections and has led to the two views on safety, 'Safety I' and 'Safety II'. 'Safety I' is defined as the absence of failure and 'Safety II' is defined as the ability to succeed under varying conditions so that the number of intended and acceptable outcomes is as high as possible (Hollnagel 2013, Wears, Hollnagel and Braithwaite 2015).

1.7.1 The Prevailing Approach to Safety

Three years ago it was without a doubt one of the key moments of my career when I had the opportunity to hear Erik Hollnagel talk about safety (2016). I sat transfixed. He talked about the use of the term safety and how people don't really describe or define it and that the danger with that is that we all think that everyone else thinks the same thing. In most cases, he said that when people think of safety they think of things going wrong and that the definition of a safe system is a system where as little as possible goes wrong. If we take that mindset then the definition of safety is therefore 'freedom from harm' and we seek a set of non-events i.e., when nothing goes wrong. This really resonated with my experience of my work in safety, which as we have seen in the previous section, has been all about understanding and measuring failure, harm and learning about why incidents and accidents happen.

Hollnagel went on to describe two contrasting views on safety. The reduction of harm through the study of failure (coined as 'Safety I') and the study of how people and systems are able to succeed under variations so that the number of intended and acceptable outcomes is as high as possible (coined as 'Safety II'). Hollnagel argues that the same behaviours and decisions that produce good care can also produce poor care. The same decisions that lead to success can also lead to failure. Behaviours or actions that can lead to making an error or mistake are variations of the same actions that produce success. It is only with the benefit of hindsight can we see that some of the decisions led to failure and some to success; however, we only study those that led to failure.

> In healthcare things are trying to be understood by looking backwards.

The predominant methodology for 'Safety I' in healthcare, as has been set out in the earlier part of the book, is to capture things that go wrong (incidents) and investigate them using root cause analysis. But, as we have seen incidents happen because of a convergence of conditions that are connected with the pursuit of success but sometimes the combination triggers failure instead. As Hollnagel and his colleagues say, the basis for patient safety cannot and should not be the cases where things go wrong, either in the sense that an accident or incident occurs, or the sense that formal quality criteria are not met. Nor should the basis be the cases where things go exceptionally well, the times we succeed but which we rarely make an effort to comprehend.

Our work in healthcare safety to date has been to focus on the outliers of the system (where it doesn't work such as incidents and where it succeeds and is considered excellent) and attempt to manage that system by addressing the outliers that are deemed to have failed and using the solutions from the outliers that are deemed to succeed.

> Rather than looking at either or both tails of a normal distribution of outcomes, we should look at the broad area in the middle, at the things that happen frequently or always, in the daily activities of the everyday clinical work that just functions and unfolds regularly as it should.
>
> **Wears, Hollnagel and Braithwaite 2015**

1.7.2 Erik Hollnagel and Resilience Engineering

The presentation led me to read anything I could get my hands on that Hollnagel had written. Hollnagel is a resilience engineer, the Chief Consultant at the Centre for Quality in Southern Denmark. He is a professor at the University of Southern Denmark and has worked in universities, research centres and industries in Denmark, England, Norway, Sweden and France. He has focused on many domains including nuclear power, aerospace and aviation, software engineering, land-based traffic and healthcare. He has published widely and is the author or editor of more than twenty books including five books on resilience engineering.

Resilience engineering emerged at the turn of the century and has since received widespread recognition. When people talk about resilience they often talk about it in terms of an individual looking after themselves, making sure that they can cope with whatever is thrown at them and to bounce back. Resilience lectures are often filled with ways in which the individual can relax or find something to take their minds of their day-to-day stresses. However, in terms of safety, it really does not mean this.

I described healthcare as a complex adaptive system in the previous section. Resilience cannot simply be the responsibility of an individual, it is much better defined as the ability of the team or the system to monitor and adjust performance to achieve its goals even when the unexpected happens (Wears, Hollnagel and Braithwaite 2015). Therefore, resilient health care can be defined as the ability of the healthcare system to adjust its functioning prior to, during or following events, changes, disturbances and opportunities. Therefore, resilience is about a different way of anticipating, monitoring, responding and learning. These are the four key areas that are required to embed resilience into the system:

■ Know what to expect – anticipate
■ Know what to look for – monitor
■ Know what to do – respond
■ Know what has happened – learn

Hollnagel's view is that patient safety is more than the absence of risk or incidents but more the ability to perform in a resilient manner. The only way it can do that is to study how health systems work and not just how they fail. His view is that the prevailing approach ('Safety I') ignores the subtleties of everyday work and ignores the reasons why it almost always goes right despite the obstacles and difficulties. 'Safety I' ignores the adaptations and adjustments that actually enable frontline people to get stuff done. The view of Hollnagel and his colleagues is that in order to improve safety or create safety what we need to do in healthcare is take a close look at the work as it takes place in everyday situations. Not the work that people think should be done, not the work that people will tell you about but the actual way in which people work including the things they may do that are not conventional or according to policy or considered the right thing to do.

1.7.3 A Different View

We must reject the notion, however well-intentioned, that the primary path to improved patient safety is to learn from failure. As Shorrock (2013) says it is a bit like 'trying to understand happiness by focusing only on rare episodes of misery'. Or as de Vos (2018) says it is a bit like 'trying to understand successful marriage by only looking at divorces'. Safety should be so much more than simply looking at failure.

> Knowledge and error flow from the same mental sources, only success can tell one from the other.
>
> **Mach 1905**

Sometimes it takes a very simple question to be asked in order to jolt us out of a way of working. In fact, sometimes simple questions can be extremely profound. For me one of the most profound questions asked of healthcare safety in recent years is:

> Why do you only look at what goes wrong?

Let us look at the statistic discussed before 'that 10% of inpatients will be harmed by the care that they receive and not the underlying illness or disease'. If we believe that statistic, however flawed it is then if 10% of things 'go wrong' then conversely 90% of things 'go right' or 'go ok' or just go. But what we do is only focus on the 10%. The 10% of things like never events, serious incidents, learning from deaths, complaints and claims are where 100% of our efforts in patient safety are placed.

The knock-on effect of this is that we change the whole system based on 10% of things going wrong rather than maybe keeping the system the same and accepting the variability because it works for 90% of the time. Or even better studying the 90% so that we may in fact increase the 90% so that in turn will lessen the 10%. Therefore, in order to truly understand how our systems, processes and even people are performing we need to study both the 10% and the 90%. This is 'Safety II'.

> It is necessary to put the focus on how health care systems succeed and stop perpetuating the myopic focus on how they fail.
>
> **Hollnagel 2016**

'Safety II' shifts us away from failure towards success. This is not just about the successes but the ways in which failure was averted. 'Safety II' suggests that in healthcare we study:

- The unexpected and emergent
- How people adjust and adapt
- How people create order out of disorder
- The inevitable and necessary performance variability

Not only should we study this, we should celebrate it. Celebrate the fact that people got through their day and things went ok. The latest thinking in safety (Vincent and Amalberti 2016, Dekker 2019, Hollnagel 2013) is the way in which we can help those people succeed under the varying conditions, understand the everyday in order to replicate and optimise what we do. Understand work-as-done in order to prevent things from going wrong. A 'Safety II' mindset, therefore, leads to the definition of safety management as a way to maintain the ability to succeed and not the prevention of accidents and incidents (Hollnagel 2013).

1.7.4 'Safety I' and 'Safety II'

'Safety II' is a combination of both 'Safety I' and 'Safety II' thinking

One of the crucial things we need to get right is that 'Safety II' does not replace 'Safety I'. Like many things in life the answer is in a balance of the two, an integration of the different thinking rather than the false binaries. 'Safety II' is 'Safety I' and 'Safety II' thinking – the two are bought together. But there is the misconception associated with 'Safety I' that it should be replaced by 'Safety II'. That it is 'Safety I' **or** 'Safety II'. But that is not the case, doing safety differently or implementing 'Safety II' is not about dismissing the past or rejecting the 'Safety I' approach. 'Safety II' is the combination of the two; keeping the practices that continue to work but abandoning or at the very least addressing the approaches, methods and tools that have been now proven to be false, myths or fallacies. The lack of progress to date is due to how 'Safety I' models have been used and applied rather than the models themselves.

'Safety I' should not be dismissed simply because it has failed; it is the way it has been implemented and continues to be done that is the problem rather than the founding principles of safety thinking.

So, as you can see Hollnagel and colleagues suggest we should study all of it; things that go *right*, and things that go *ok* together with when it goes *wrong*. It is not an' either or' – it is not binary. In that respect, earlier in the book I referenced the work of Pinker (2017) who has a much more factually optimistic view of the world than most. With a nod to 'Safety I' and 'Safety II', he goes on to say it does not mean that things do not go wrong, and it does not mean that they are acceptable because more things go right. It is still important to know and focus on these things but there needs to be a much more balanced (negative and positive) approach.

There are those that are concerned that people are dismissing the needs of the individuals that suffer as a result of poor safety in favour of looking at success. But as Pinker says, the 'success' still represents people, it represents large numbers of people. Again it is the balance of caring for both the patients that have suffered harm and the patients that have recovered or been treated safely, compassionately and effectively.

In so many aspects of life our experiences are richer than they were 30–40 years ago but there appears to be a moral weight on people to expose what can go wrong (Pinker 2017). If we ask the question; 'what is the thing that went wrong today?' then that leads to unintended consequences of focusing on negativity and failure. This question is all too easy to ask because one can pick out single or memorable events that have failed rather than the ongoing and frequent times things succeed. It is not news if it goes ok and the same things happen year on year even if year on year it is getting better. But when something goes wrong or fails it is easy to be singled out. The impression the reader or watcher or patient gets is things are getting worse which in fact is not reality.

This emerging view of safety has captured the imagination of people who work in safety in healthcare. This is in part because of the overwhelming feeling that if we keep doing the same things in safety we will not be making the difference we all want. There is also a huge desire to shift from the relentless focus on the negative and the things that have gone wrong. 'Safety II' provides us with a different lens with which to look at how the safety of patient care could be improved.

1.7.5 How Do We Do It?

One of the questions people ask me about 'Safety II' is how do we do this when we are snowed under doing 'Safety I'. If we are already drowning in data why would we want to add more? That is where the myth comes in that it is all about rejecting 'Safety I' and moving to 'Safety II'. To 'do' 'Safety II' we do not have to move away from the approaches we have used to date but we do need to be much better at using our current strategies. We do need to rethink how we capture 'Safety I' data and how much effort we spend on 'Safety I' and then think about how we can free up that time to focus on 'Safety II' data.

> Safety differently is not blindly following a stepping stone path but taking the time to turn over each stone and challenging why is the stone here in the first place, what was the intent, it is still valid and useful.
>
> **Wong 2015**

People are energised by 'Safety II'. They, like me, have read or heard Hollnagel or Dekker speak and are eager to make this real. They want to go from being inspired to seeing it implemented but as Dekker says they want to waste no time on any further understanding or effort (Dekker 2018). He says people want the answer to 'what do I do now?' People want someone to tell them what to do because they don't have the time to think or to study it further. They just want to be told what to do.

There is often this dilemma which is 'please don't instruct me or tell me what to do' but 'tell me what to do'. As Dekker says this is 'literally taking a safety I mind-set to a safety II world' (2018). His view is that providing a step by step guide to 'Safety II' would negate what this new thinking is all about because it isn't a checklist or a downloadable solution. 'Safety II' is a whole new way of thinking that needs to be experienced and lived. It is a way of being curious about how the system functions and how people adapt and adjust, it is a series of questions and conversations, it is a look at people's worlds in a very different way. This is a change in behaviour far more than a new tool or technique.

Wong (2018) asks 'do we need a recipe follower or a chef? He says anyone can follow a recipe if they are well written and easily followed and practice and expertise will increase success. He says there are a lot of recipes in 'Safety I'. What happens, however, if you don't have all the recipe ingredients or someone demands that you must cut the baking time in half or that the recipe follower is tired, confused and pressured? If you keep trying to follow the recipe with these changes in dynamics and conditions then you may fail. A chef however adapts to the unexpected conditions, doesn't always follow the cookbook but knows the art and principles of cooking (Wong 2018). 'Safety II' enables people to become chefs rather than simply following the recipe.

'Safety II' means we can seek to understand how things mostly go right as an explanation for how things sometimes go wrong. It helps us understand that all performance ultimately flows from the same underlying processes and systems with the same behaviours and practices. It provides us with a way to hear stories of success and to appreciate the times when nothing went wrong. This is a much more proactive approach to safety that has emerged from a substantial theoretical foundation; decades of research in safety, human factors, sociology, psychology, cognitive systems engineering, organisation complexity and resilience engineering (Hollnagel et al. 2013).

What we should be doing is studying successful marriages in order to keep them successful and hopefully prevent the divorce.

In order to help there are a number of emerging models which are being tried and tested to turn the theory into practice and help 'bring to life' 'Safety II' which are found in Part Two of the book.

1.8 Part One Summary

Part One describes the growing sense of unease about the way we do safety in healthcare together with some exciting ways in which we can do it differently. From as far back as 1850 we have focused on harm and failure and in particular people have tried to understand why people die. To understand the scale and nature of harm the vast majority of the studies have concentrated on acute care and inpatients in hospitals. This has led to the claim that around one in ten patients experience some type of health-related harm while receiving inpatient care. But this was based on subjective reviews of incomplete case notes. In truth, no one really knows the true scale of the problem.

The response to these studies has been to capture more data; set up incident reporting systems and investigate a few of them further. Organisations have been encouraged to collect as much data as possible which is why we are now drowning in poor quality data. The investigations are an industry and are conducted by people who are not trained to investigate complex systems or trained to identify the potential solutions that could reduce the things that fail. All of these methods are surrounded by a culture of blame and fear. In summary, we have failed to effectively learn and in many cases failed to improve the safety of patient care despite all these efforts. This predominant approach is coined as 'Safety I'.

However, creating a balanced approach to safety does not mean we have to dismiss everything that we have done to date. 'Safety I' should not be rejected simply because it has failed; it is the way it has been implemented and continues to be done that is the problem rather than the founding principles of safety thinking. So, crucially, the issue is with implementation and not necessarily the strategies we have been using. However, we really have to get better at using what we currently have and getting rid of the things that frankly do not work or are making things worse.

The alternative view set out here is to shift our focus from purely studying failure and to think about how we work on a daily basis, how we can learn from when things work, and when they don't. This has been coined as 'Safety II' or 'safety differently' or the 'new view' (Hollnagel 2013, Dekker 2018). In order to truly understand how our systems, processes and how people are performing in healthcare we need to study both the 10% of times that it goes wrong and the 90% of times it goes right. We should study all of it.

We have seen how complexity science forces us to consider the dynamic and non-dynamic properties of healthcare and the varying characteristics, forces, variables and influences across it that need to allow people to operate successfully within a constantly changing and unpredictable environment (Mannion and Braithwaite 2017). We have seen how some areas of healthcare are predictable and certain and some 'normally' unpredictable and uncertain (Vincent and Amalberti 2016). So we need strategies and interventions and solutions that are fit for purpose – the right ones for the right level from simple, to complicated and to complex. The right ones for the particular area of healthcare.

The answer is in a balance of the two 'Safety I' and 'Safety II', together with an integration of the concepts and ideas from the three models of safety and complex adaptive systems. In my view, healthcare safety should urgently integrate both 'Safety I' and 'Safety II' if we are to see the full picture of safety. Integration of our thinking, feeling and behaviour associated with both as ignoring one over the other or falsely separating them misses the point. To study the conditions that lead to failure and to study the conditions that allow safety to emerge will provide us with the answers to how we can help people work safely.

If we want to change or improve or strengthen a complex system we need to look for patterns in the behaviour of a system, we cannot simply use linear cause and effect methods and we need to look for interconnections within the system rather than the isolated problems. I recommend that by bringing these components together it will help us understand the dynamic nature of the healthcare system, the relationships, the connections and the way in which care is delivered which is dependent upon the interconnections and interactions that make it possible.

The ideal balanced approach to safety therefore is both reactive and proactive approaches, and through studying both failure and success. This new approach to safety has emerged from a substantial theoretical foundation; decades of research in safety, human factors, sociology, psychology, cognitive systems engineering, organisation complexity and resilience engineering.

My proposition is that if we are going to do things differently then we need to go beyond the traditional science associated with safety to subjects such as behavioural economics, resilience engineering, just culture, kindness, gratitude, joy in work, respect, humility, positive deviance and positive emotions. We need to pay attention to the number of safety experts who have been sharing their knowledge about what we could do differently over the last decade; Shorrock, Hollnagel, Braithwaite, Mannion, Vincent, Amalberti, Shojania, Dixon-Woods, Berwick and Dekker to name a few. These people have triggered an emergent view that the prevailing approach to safety needs a rethink. All of which provides us with a new exciting and joyful approach to safety which could truly transform the way in which we can finally help the people in healthcare to work as safely as they can.

1.9 Part One Actions

A few actions to help you create a balanced approach to
safety:

■ Understand the limitations of safety measurement and, in
  particular, case note reviews. You will never be able to
  measure everything. Incident reporting systems are not
  a measure of your organisational safety or the safety of a
  particular unit, practice or team so instead find the things
  you can count with a degree of certainty and think about
  what you want to measure that demonstrates learning.
■ Think about how your organisation or department or
  team anticipates, monitors, responds and learns about
  things happening within the workplace.
■ Review the major causes of preventable healthcare-related
  harm to estimate associated increased mortality e.g.,
  deaths associated with venous thromboembolism, surgical
  complications or hospital-acquired infections.
■ Combine outcome with process measures to increase
  specificity when identifying preventable deaths, e.g.,
  measuring pulmonary embolism in patients who die and
  who did not receive adequate venous thromboembolism
  measures.
■ Understand the limitations of both incident reporting and
  incident investigation – be armed with knowledge when
  people ask you what your strategy is for collecting, counting and learning.
■ Use incident reporting systems for incidents which have
  the potential for learning.
■ Document your strategy for what you will collect via
  an incident reporting system and what you will collect
  using other data collection systems in order to reduce the
  amount of data in a reporting system. This will free the
  system up so that you can use it more easily for learning

rather than counting. If you want to count then simply use a spreadsheet or table.

- Lots of data can be captured via alternative methods of collection e.g., falls and pressure ulcers can be simply recorded on a simple Excel spreadsheet and counted over time with the detail of what happened placed in the patients' notes. The efforts that it takes to complete a form and the subsequent investigation can be shifted towards the efforts of preventing patients from falling or developing pressure ulcers rather than counting when they do.
- Be ready with your case for those that will scrutinise you and want to know why you are not collecting certain information via an incident reporting system – make sure that you make the case for learning rather than counting.
- Increase the skills of investigators and only use people who are experts in incident investigation. This will ensure that the reports are of high quality and will be able to go beyond the superficial review and recommendations.
- Train your investigators in appreciative inquiry techniques and ensure they understand the restorative just culture when investigating incidents, complaints or claims – ensure that all investigations include appreciative inquiry questions such as 'what went well?' and 'what did people do to make this as safe as it could have been?'
- Ensure your strategy encourages quality reports rather than pressuring people with speed or quantity.
- Reduce the expectations in terms of finding the root cause, which are rarely found – focus on the contributory factors and causal factors that go beyond simply telling people to stop making mistakes or to communicate better.
- Look to study groups of incidents in order to understand the things that are consistent throughout the incidents and address these rather than one incident at a time.
- Write a very short number (3–5) of meaningful and implementable recommendations.

■ Consider how you can integrate both 'Safety I' and 'Safety II' to see the full picture of safety – this will mean thinking about how you spend less effort focused on failure and more time and resources on thinking about work-as-done and success.

■ Reduce the time you spend on failure in favour of understanding how work-as-done and how things go well in order to build a picture of safety.

■ Investigate care, a case, a shift, a task or a day that went well and identify the points that you would like to replicate time and time again for the future and seek to understand how things mostly go right as an explanation for how things sometimes go wrong.

■ When investigating both failure and success ask people what adjustments did they make in order to keep their patients safe – these are the gold nuggets that you want to learn about.

■ Understand complexity and its impact on healthcare and try out the methods to understand work-as-done (described later in this book) and use the understanding of complexity to build your approach to a different way of doing safety.

■ Consider how your organisation or department is structured – does it lend itself to distributed leadership and devolved decision making?

■ Create a plan of your organisation and identify which areas are ultra-safe, which are high-reliability and which are ultra-adaptive. Then set out to develop the different bespoke models and structures that will support the success of these different areas.

■ If you want to know how safe your system is, study the properties and characteristics of the entire system; the dynamics, the independent and interdependent relationships that make up the system, and the emergent behaviours of the system.

Part Two

Turn the Theory
into Practice

To help the WHOLE SYSTEM
perform well, we need to help
all INDIVIDUALS perform well.

2.1 Part Two Introduction

Part Two focuses on the theories and concepts described in Part One and explores how we can turn these into practice, i.e., how we can practically use them to improve the safety of patient care. It will explore the methods for studying daily work – often referred to as 'work-as-done'. The different approaches here will help us actually notice the things we don't notice and reflect on the non-events and the things we take for granted every day from morning to night because they work just as they should. It will share the work of Hollnagel, Shorrock and Mesman and others who are exploring the different approaches that can bring the new safety concepts to life. I will also share the developing method of functional resonance analysis; a new way of measuring and monitoring safety using an exciting framework developed by Vincent, Burnett and Carthey (2013). It will culminate in how I believe that in order to progress we need to address the language we use; changing the language to change the mindset in relation to safety.

2.2 Implementation

2.2.1 What Is Implementation?

Implementation is the complex process of turning policy or theory into practice. It is the multiple steps required to take a piece of research or a good idea, or good practice and turn it into action. If the good idea is picked up or adopted by individuals and then used on a day-to-day basis it is then said to be embedded. If the good idea is then shared across to other individuals it is described as spread. If the good idea sticks and people continue to be different as a result it is said to be sustained. Implementation, therefore, is the combined process of dissemination, adoption, embedding, spread and sustainability of good ideas. It takes, on average, 17 years to turn 14% of original research findings into practice and there is a sustainability failure rate of up to 70% of organisational change (Woodward 2008).

There is a growing science of implementation. This is the study of methods to promote the systematic uptake of research findings and other evidence-based practices into routine practice. Implementation science draws mainly from the disciplines of evidence-based medicine and guidance implementation, together with the diffusion of innovations, change management, organisational development and behavioural change theories. This field now has an evidence base that informs people about the core components of implementation and implementation practice (Woodward 2008). It is about studying each aspect of implementation plus the reasons for the gap between ideas and practice; understanding how to narrow or bridge this gap (Woodward 2008).

It is easy to have an idea or design a device or write a guideline that should work if implemented. The hard part is to take the idea, device or guideline and make it work well every time. Yet, who has not attended a conference focused on quality or safety and not been frustrated with the comments; 'Let's create a new policy', or 'create a checklist', or 'why is it so hard for people to simply do the right thing'. This over-simplistic model of implementation is characterised by 'why don't they just do it'. This model assumes that once the idea or solution has been designed, then the staff will simply carry out the actions required.

Implementation requires thoughtful action, expertise and effort and there is no easy way of doing it. I learned that each stage, dissemination, adoption, embedding, spread and sustainability requires special thought. I learned all about the many factors or principles that can be used in order to maximise the chances of the good idea being finally sustained. Very few get it right; effective implementation of knowledge, research and information into healthcare practice remains for many an unconquered challenge. Implementation is a slow and haphazard process (Woodward 2008).

At every stage of the process people can and do get it wrong. It is not nearly as simple as people think. Implementation needs dedicated resources, funding and time and a shift away from the short-term approach to change and implementation. It is a fantasy to think that an idea can be implemented through to sustained change in just three to five years. This is in part because implementation requires a culture shift; a culture whereby the embedded idea it still used even when politics, or policies or people change. Understanding the simple reality that implementation takes times is important but we can also aim to reduce the time from the average of 17 years.

2.2.2 *Implementation and Healthcare*

In healthcare, the traditional approach to implementation is to simply disseminate the good idea and expect the 'audience' to pick it up and run with it. The approach with guidance or alerts is mainly one of distribution to a passive group of people who may not even notice that it has arrived. The approach of relying on passive diffusion of information to inform health professionals about safer practices, is doomed to failure in a global environment in which well over two million articles on clinical issues are published annually (Woodward 2008).

In patient safety there are lots of good ideas about keeping patients safer or reducing harm. There are the large top-down interventions but implementation is not always about making a large change; in fact it is often about making small incremental changes that can make things easier, better, more effective and safer. It is in fact sometimes easier to make changes because of a defining moment. Making changes after a major incident or a catastrophe has a stronger chance of success because of the motivation caused by the incident itself. The harder thing to do is to convince people to change on a daily basis. To consider every small decision made and ask whether that decision could have been a better one. It is also harder to convince people to change if they don't see a significant and large change. Visible outcomes are always great motivators whether you want to lose weight or reduce the number of falls or pressure ulcers. Seeing the graph go down or the weight go off are great ways in which to convince people to continue. What if you can't see them? Most changes are notearth-shattering improvements that everyone will want to talk about and share. However, improving in a small way is meaningful. The difficulty here is noticing whether there is a difference over time and being able to recognise it enough to continue to do the same thing.

National bodies in the UK in particular love to create standards, alerts and 'must do' notices and targets. There have been repeated alerts published and disseminated in relation to the same topics in healthcare. This should tell us that the method of 'telling people just to do it' isn't working. For example, in the UK there have been multiple alerts issued over the last fifteen years to try to prevent patients from dying as a result of the insertion of a nasogastric tube into the lungs instead of the stomach. The people on the receiving end are expected to implement these quickly often with very little resources to help. What implementation scientists tell us is that guidelines or standards or alerts issued in isolation rarely change people's individual practice (Woodward 2008). They are, at best, complied with, but they have not been found to drive sustained improvement. This is the gap between what we assume improves patient safety and what is actually done in practice.

Therefore, in healthcare we are drowning in ways in which we could improve; numerous interventions and solutions exist, as well as lots of research and guidance (Carthey et al. 2011). Carthey and colleagues have described the unintended consequences of this as follows. The volume is challenging with a constant barrage of guidelines which lessens their impact and reduces compliance with the more important ones. There are multiple polices and guidelines for the same topic. They are hard to access and have confusing titles, as well as some being extremely long and wordy.

2.2.3 What Can We Do Differently?

We can study implementation science to support patient safety science and focus on the delivery of appropriate safety policy, recommendations, research, and theory so that it is adopted, spread and embedded into everyday practice. Implementation can never be a passive process. To choose to move to a new practice means that people have to give up on the old practice. However if the perception is that the old practice is just fine, then what is the incentive? A primary aim should be to demonstrate there is an explicit need for the change or the solution and that the proposed solution is the right one for the context and problem. Carthey and colleagues suggest that staff may break the rules because they are so hard to comply with. They recommend:

■ Cooperation and collaboration at a national level (from the policy setters) to reduce the burden.
■ Local organisations need to review existing policies and consider whether volume, version control, accessibility, length, or titling problems may increase the risk of non-compliance.
■ Human factors science should be applied to the development, design and testing of policies and guidelines; involving healthcare staff who have to follow the policy in the development phase will ensure they are usable in practice.
■ Rather than sending the draft policy to a small group of experts to comment on, trusts should carry out walkthroughs and risk assessments aimed at identifying how the policy could be read and misinterpreted by those who have to use it.

■ Trusts should also learn from research on implementing initiatives and evidence-based medicine. The principles for getting clinicians to implement evidence-based medicine also apply to improving levels of procedural compliance.
  – If a clinician is aware of the evidence and the benefits, and if the implementation process is practical it is more likely to be adopted.
  – If healthcare professionals can see the need for a policy or guideline, if it is written in a way that shows a practical understanding of the real world, and if it is easy to access and follow, staff are more likely to comply with it.
■ Finally, both national and local organisations would benefit from adopting tracking mechanisms used by industries such as air traffic control which enable them to monitor whether staff have read and, more importantly, understood key messages.

The authors conclude that

> clinical policies and guidelines are undoubtedly an essential foundation of high-quality patient care. However, their extraordinary and uncoordinated proliferation in the NHS confuses staff, causes inefficiencies and delay, and is becoming a threat to patient safety. We need to recognise the problems caused by current approaches and introduce greater rationalisation and standardisation at both national and local levels.

Implementation science and *Safety II* have one key thing in common. Those designing the interventions or guidance that they want to implement must be aware of the impact that they are making. They must seek to understand work-as-done and get beneath the surface of what is going on every day. But, every day the 'everyday' gets in the way of noticing anything new. How do we help people to notice the things they need, when they may only have five minutes in their day to sit down and look beyond their daily activity? One key way of doing this is to be much less directive. Instead of prescribing steps people could be left up to themselves to adapt and own the intervention or solution. Lilford argues for a more minimalist approach as a default (2017). Fit the intervention within their system but do not force it. There is no one size fits all. He argues that contexts differ and as a result people need to vary their actions from place to place, just as a cook must improvise in the kitchen. Trying to fix all these different variables in advance may 'limit room for manoeuvre and may even be demotivating'. Additionally, as I have argued many times, attempting a description of an intervention that encompasses every component to be used in practice is a completely unrealistic task; it sets people up to fail and even worse, punishes them when they do so.

2.3 Narrow the Gap between Work-as-Imagined and Work-as-Done

The terms work-as-imagined and work-as-done help to convey the way that people *think* about how work is done and the wacy the work is *actually done* (Hollnagel 2017). Here I will look at models that try to find out 'how' things normally work, how they happen as a routine and what also goes well. These models ask the people who are performing the task or procedure or work about the adjustments they have made to make things work. Because while people struggle to remember why or how things go well they tend to remember the adjustments they have had to make because they have to consciously think about making the adjustment. There are ways in which we can tap into this memory. First, let's explore the theories.

2.3.1 Work-as-Done

The things that happen frequently in the daily activities of everyday clinical work has been coined as work-as-done. Work-as-done consists of adaptations and adjustments by healthcare practitioners in order to keep people safe. Healthcare workers at the frontline of healthcare adapt and adjust their actions and decisions according to the patients they are caring for, the conditions they work in and the situations they face, the combination of which are rarely if ever the same. In general, work-as-done is the real conditions that people are working in, the 'messy reality' as Shorrock (2017) would say. In order for a system to be understood it is necessary to know what goes on 'inside it'. Understanding how things are done when nothing goes wrong is a prerequisite for understanding how they may fail.

2.3.2 Work-as-Imagined

However, conventionally we assume that people will work as they are supposed to and may not even explore how they actually work. This is the difference between work-as-done and work-as-imagined. The term work-as-imagined refers to the way people who regulate, inspect and design interventions don't really understand what reality is actually like. The distinction between the two is often used to point out that there may be a considerable difference between what people are assumed or expected to do and what they actually do. The policy makers, regulators and others believe they know what happens or should happen and if there is a difference between this opinion the people involved are accused of non-compliance, violations or performance deviation.

Also, if people who are responsible for developing guidelines or standards or policies and procedures are relying on what they imagine someone does rather than what the frontline workers actually do then the policy could turn out to be unworkable, incomplete or fundamentally wrong. And in respect to safety solutions, if the designers don't understand, consult and engage the frontline then they can develop the wrong solutions that won't work. If they think they have come up with something that 'will solve the problems at the frontline' and those who are at the frontline are left with the feeling that 'this doesn't solve our problems', it feels clumsy. The incongruence makes it hard for frontline staff to implement things they are being told to do, resulting in frustration and workarounds. The unintended consequence of this is that it triggers a degree of initiative fatigue or fatigue in relation to initiatives that seem misaligned with the goals of their day-to-day work, creating a chasm between the leadership and frontline of organisations.

> When we fix the wrong thing for the wrong reason the same problems continue to surface. It's costly and demoralising.
>
> **Brown 2018**

2.3.3 Work-as-Prescribed

There will always be a desire to prescribe the way care is delivered or improved or changed. Work-as-prescribed is when we set clear rules and detailed instructions for carrying out tasks. If this is a requirement then we need to figure out how people can prescribe much more precisely in a way that helps people work. In the three models of safety, I shared the work of Vincent and Amalberti who assert that there are some specialties such as radiotherapy, chemotherapy and medication administration (the ultra-safe) when the gap between work-as-done and work-as-prescribed needs to be as narrow as it possibly could be. This is where it is vital that the prescribed practice matches reality and is constantly reviewed to ensure that it continues to do so. Some forms of prescribed work become defunct but are still officially in place. Some forms of prescribed work have drifted into mythology with people convinced that they are expected to work in a certain way which has in fact never been prescribed.

> Just because it is common sense, it doesn't mean it is common practice.

Guidance in the form of standards, procedures, checklists, alerts, interventions and policies are necessary in healthcare and are here to stay. However, if there is a serious attempt to make rules for every aspect of the work in healthcare, people will soon realise that it is impossible to explain every single action for every possible environment and situation. Therefore, if we are going to make them workable then we need to ensure that they match the day-to-day activity as closely as possible, which is intuitively easy to do and in fact enhances and optimises everyday behaviour. Even if the guidance (of whatever form it takes) is developed by people who used to be those that were at the frontline and immersed in the work-as-done, the moment they step out of that area they start to become removed from it. Healthcare delivery and healthcare treatments are changing all of the time and people's memories become distorted.

However, most work-as-done in ultra-adaptive healthcare is impossible to prescribe exactly. Work-as-done in these areas is a combination of experience, expertise, clinical judgement and know-how. Not everything we do in ultra-adaptive environments can be written down in detail. In this case, the guidance is more likely to work if it is written in general terms rather than with fine detail which may not quite fit with reality. It is important to ensure that the guidance is constantly reviewed to ensure that it is still up to date and also still workable.

2.3.4 Work-as-Disclosed

Work-as-disclosed is how people describe what they do either in writing or when we talk to each other. However this may not always be what is actually done. For many reasons, it may be the partial truth. This may be because:

- Explaining every little detail would be too tedious.
- We do things automatically and we may forget some of the details when we come to explain it.
- We may tailor it to the audience and when we come to explain it we do it too simply.
- We say what we want people to hear.

A surprising finding of Ariely (2012) is that humans lie (to ourselves and others) every ten minutes. So in a culture of fear and when we are being scrutinised we may 'just tell people what should happen not what does happen' or 'simply tell people what we think they want to hear'. In addition, work as disclosed may be different for different people involved in the same incident.

Everyone involved will have their own unique experience and account of what happened, which may differ and even be contradictory. No one will be either right or wrong just different depending upon what they recall, what part they played or their experience. Bringing together all the truths provides a fuller picture.

Nurses, in particular, often do not report workarounds and conceal the actual practices they do to keep patients safe. Staff confronted with ever-increasing imposed demands are frantically resorting to workarounds just to survive a shift. In that respect, those designing safety interventions may think that the interventions are working when they are not because no one is disclosing that they are not. This means that interventions continue to be churned out which then lead to more and more workarounds. Ironically, as the number of workarounds increases the organisation becomes more and more complex.

Work-as-disclosed is a particular issue for healthcare.

The fact that something may not be disclosed relates to the fear of what people would do and say if they realised what actually happened on a day-to-day basis to get things done. It is also scary for someone to understand that you may not be as perfect as people expect you to be. For example, if we asked those that work in healthcare whether they wash their hands in between every patient, most if not all will say yes. They will say yes because anything else is declaring that you are 'unhygienic', 'uncaring', 'slapdash' or a 'sub-human being' because you could not even be bothered to wash your hands between patients. However, in the real world some people may not wash their hands for all sorts of reasons. You will only know those reasons if you ask the question in a way that people can genuinely feel that they can disclose that they don't do it all the time. You can only ask the question if you have a culture where people will not feel judged and will feel that someone cares even if they answer no. You can only ask the question if you are willing to listen, learn and then figure out what could be done to help people wash their hands more often.

2.3.5 *The Problems with Inspection*

Inspection comes in many forms but is very much related to 'Safety I' – predominantly retrospective and focused on things that go wrong. These forms include clinical audit, incident reporting data, outcome data, internal investigations, external inspections from a regulatory body and external inquiries. Healthcare over the last two decades has been the subject of much scrutiny from inquiry to inquiry which can have a serious impact on safety.

There are different views as to who should 'judge' or inspect others. Inspection is often carried out by people who are not from the area or the unit they are inspecting. Dekker (2010) believes that we should aim for the inspectors to be experts, who can truly understand the work and help to understand the gaps. They should do this with a sense of humility and realism that they may never truly understand what happened or why people did what they did or do what they do. Those working in human factors and ergonomics consciously try to understand and explain the gaps between the varieties of work to help improve system performance and human wellbeing, without unintentionally bringing about harm along the way (Shorrock 2017).

Asking questions during inspections or investigations might even temporarily halt the workarounds and improvisations (work-as-done) because people fear that they will be noticed. This could continue until no one is looking. It also may, in turn, have a knock on effect on the safety of patient care because the workarounds were in fact needed to get stuff done and keep people safe. One could suggest that inspections rather than help improve safety could, in fact, be making things worse.

In fact inappropriate adherence to the plan or directives or rules in certain circumstances could put both staff and patients at risk. For example, the patient that collapses in the car park outside a hospital may well need to be resuscitated by staff who have no infection prevention equipment. The rules may say that gloves should be worn, hands washed, protective airway equipment should be used. The reality is that there are no gloves, an inability to wash hands and no airway equipment. The staff at this point are 'required' to violate the organisation's infection prevention policies in order to try and save a patient's life.

When things do not appear to be getting any better (based on 'Ssafety I' measures) inspection (external and internal) creates more pressure on the leadership and frontline of an organisation. More policies are issued, more interventions are disseminated and more people are told to stop making mistakes. What is needed is a reduction in the regulatory regime, the imposed bureaucracy and the insistence on compliance with rules and procedures that are not fit for purpose. Instead, focus on outcomes such as learning and building on what is working.

2.3.6 Why Is It Important to Narrow the Gap?

It is important to narrow the gap because safety must be based on an understanding of work-as-done, an understanding of the everyday. Constraining performance adjustments or shifting people's actions towards a working practice which does not fit with this everyday will make work difficult or impossible and even lead to failure. In order to narrow the gap the policy makers or designers need to understand the conditions and how people behave, what happens under certain situations and what happens when the conditions change? It is especially important to consider the dynamics, different parts and the dependencies in complex adaptive systems such as healthcare.

It is essential to study work-as-done because we should realise that whenever something goes wrong it rarely if ever happens for the first time. Whatever happens has happened or been done many times before and will in all likelihood be done again many times in the future. It is also true to say this applies for when something goes right. It has been done many times before and will be done many times again for the simple reason that it works.

Wears, Hollnagel and Braithwaite 2015

2.4 Models to Understand Work-as-Done

Studying work-as-done in healthcare includes times when we simulate a major incident or we do simulations of tasks and procedures. These methods are used to attempt to enable greater clarity and accuracy under stressful circumstances. They seek to find out how people work under pressure, when they can be overwhelmed. This can result in bad decisions and bad behaviours that are not made through a lack of skill or innate judgement: they are made because of an inability to handle pressure at the pivotal moment. We need to test how people work simultaneously with other people, how they have to compromise, how they can learn about what life is like for them. However, they are not often used to simply understand the day-to-day work of healthcare. We don't use them to understand the work-as-done.

We have not studied work-as-done because we don't have the time and resources to do so, mainly because we are focusing all of our efforts looking at failure.

While in a complex adaptive system such as healthcare it would be virtually impossible for anyone to truly understand how all of the work is actually carried out everywhere, we need to learn as much as we can about it. In many areas of healthcare no two days are the same and there are many ways in which the work can be done. We do not have the ability to see things through other people's eyes – we see through our own eyes but we can ask and listen. The first stage of learning is listening; listening with intent, listening with the mindset of wanting to learn. There are a number of methods or models that can help us with this. They can help us learn about the everyday, the way other people work and learn about the complex adaptive system that is healthcare, how it adapts to changes, how it deals with challenges, conflicts, or unexpected circumstances. Although they are still in their infancy, the following are five potential ways to study work-as-done in healthcare:

- Ethnography and simulation
- Positive Deviance
- Exnovation
- Golden days and lives saved
- Functional Resonance analysis Method (FRAM) – described in the following section

The next section provides a brief overview of these ways with references for you to study them in more depth.

2.4.1 Ethnography and Simulation

Frontline workers may not even recognise or notice how they work and the adjustments they make on a daily basis because it is habit and they have learned to live with them in order to get things done. Ethnography is a way of observing things that happen every day. Ethnographic research can be used to study what happens all of the time rather than what happens rarely by simply observing day-to-day practice in a particular area. It is usually immersive. By studying everyday performance in this way, we can detect the small actions, decisions or adjustments and in this respect, we can try to replicate those that optimise the conditions in which people work to help them make these small changes safely.

Ethnography helps us then identify the small improvements we could make in everyday performance. Small improvements are best for sustainable change in the long term rather than larger improvements which are often too sweeping or transformational. Successful change is more likely to be about a thousand little things than one big change. One caveat for ethnography is that as is commonly known in research and in particularly ethnography, behaviours change when they are being watched let alone inspected, people change their behaviours to match what they think people want to see.

A form of ethnography is simulation. Simulation training is an experiential form of learning which helps people think about how they work day-to-day, how they can work together safely, how they build relationships and then also how they role model the behaviours outside of the simulation training. Simulation can change the dynamics of the team from being passive to proactively thinking how they work together and how people can be helped to speak up. Crucially, simulation training and the subsequent briefings create the space and opportunity for people to talk to each other about how they work.

2.4.2 Positive Deviance

Positive deviance is another way in which the ideology of Safety II can be progressed. A positive deviance approach seeks to identify and learn from those who demonstrate exceptional performance (Baxter et al. 2019). It looks at the variations in performance and processes that result in good outcomes rather than poor outcomes or harm. Those that have studied positive deviance believe it can also be used to understand and recognise the complexity of healthcare, the uncertainty and the time pressures and resource constraints of the everyday. The hypothesis behind this model is that by seeking and studying groups or individuals who perform exceptionally well and the instances when things go right, methods for best practice can be identified and disseminated to improve wider performance (Lawton et al. 2014).

Positive deviance is also based on the opinion that in every community there are certain individuals or groups whose uncommon behaviours and strategies enable them to find better solutions to problems than their peers, while having access to the same resources and facing similar or worse challenges (Lawton et al. 2014). These individuals or groups may already know what is going wrong but also what they do to prevent things from going wrong (work-as-done) and that if given the freedom to act and the freedom to generate solutions it may improve uptake and increase the likelihood of success. Lawton and her colleagues have found that positively deviant groups have leaders who encourage local ownership and plan the implementation of change which echo the mindset of 'Safety II' and complex adaptive systems. Positive deviance also recommends genuine, meaningful and constructive praise, and a positive message to balance the widespread negativity. The steps for looking at positive deviance in your organisation are to:

■ Identify the positive deviants in your organisation.
■ Study them in depth using qualitative methodology.
■ Generate hypotheses as to what could be done to achieve successes and test these hypotheses while working in partnership with those who will be subjected to any new practices.

Now is the time to be much more supportive of those at the frontline; focusing on the behaviours, processes and systems that contribute to safer care rather than solely focus on things that detract from safer care.

Lawton 2014

Baxter and colleagues conducted research with 70 multi-disciplinary staff on eight wards to identify positive deviant success factors (2019). The authors found:

- Staff on positively deviant wards were passionate about the importance of knowing one another, as it helped them to support one another to deliver safe patient care.
- Friendly, personal connections between staff members were perceived to facilitate communication, influence their ability to contribute different perspectives, encourage them to work beyond silos and to be more broadly involved in patient care.
- Adopting *a multidisciplinary approach* and working collaboratively was discussed extensively across all wards; however, positively deviant ward staff were more emphatic about its importance.
- Everyone's contributions were encouraged and valued; staff felt listened to, were actively involved in ward activities and were kept informed of the bigger picture rather than just being told essential information. This created a shared awareness about a patient's care plan and the risks they faced, and it engendered a sense of responsibility towards patients and the team.
- Positively deviant wards particularly emphasised the importance of involving non-professional staff (e.g., healthcare assistants and domestics) in ward activities such as meetings/briefings, quality improvement projects and documentation.
- Positively deviant wards described an extremely integrated way of *working together*, which happened throughout the day and involved staff from different professional groups and levels of experience. Staff worked beyond silos contributing to multiple aspects of patient care and they trusted one another's judgements.
- Positively deviant ward staff *felt able to ask questions or for help* and stressed the emotional impact of feeling

comfortable to approach others without concern. This ensured that problems were raised with the wider team and it enabled information to be checked immediately and/or passed on to others without delay.

In total, 14 positively deviant characteristics relating to the cultural and social context of the ward were identified on medical wards for older people (Baxter et al 2019), for example:

- Integrated multidisciplinary teams
- High-performing clinical microsystems
- Overcoming professional silos, hierarchies and distributed teams
- Relational coordination – relationships based on shared knowledge, goals and mutual respect
- Positive safety culture
- Psychological safety
- Shared mental models underpinning effective teamwork

It is well recognised that *how* staff do things, and the environment or context within which they do it, are equally as important as *what* staff do.

Baxter et al. 2019

The authors found no 'silver bullets' to achieving exceptionally safe patient care and that their study rightly raises questions about the lens we apply to improvement and suggests that focus should also be dedicated to improving the cultural contexts that underpin a range of safety outcomes. The findings of this most recent research (Baxter 2019) is hugely synergistic with the discussions later in this book when I will describe the importance of caring for the people that care and the importance of things like kindness, joy, relationships and patient safety.

2.4.3 Exnovation

Exnovation is also cited as a methodology to enable compliance with 'Ssafety II' and to studying work-as-done. The term exnovation in industry is used to describe when products and processes that have been tested and confirmed to be the best are standardised to ensure that they are not innovated further. It is the philosophy of 'not innovating' further. It challenges the dominant trend of ignoring the existing practices in current improvement processes (Mesman 2016). In relation to safety, we appear to be constantly searching for new interventions, a new change, something different instead of valuing and studying what we already have. This is a very powerful way of dispelling the myth that we need to constantly change in order to get it right. Professor Jessica Mesman uses the definition from Iedema et al. (2013) to describe exnovation as 'innovation from within'. In a way, she says that this is a 'form of innovation' which is not about change, but more about observation, exploration and articulation of 'what is'.

Exnovation is further defined by Professor Jessica Mesman (2016) as 'the way to say new things about the familiar'. For example, she says, think about when you have guests over. You start to notice the mess, the stains, the things that are not as perfect as you would like. You notice it because you will have new people coming to see your home. Before that you didn't notice it, it was simply the background of your life. Mesman uses exnovation as a way to make people aware of what they do, what they say and how they practice – to study established practices and help to somehow pay attention to the invisible and to the competencies that we forget because we use them every day (Mesman 2016).

The ordinary is an extraordinary accomplishment.

Mesman 2016

Similar to ethnography and simulation training, exnovation uses video to help people pay attention to the mundane, to the implicit local routines, to what is in place in their workplace. Mesman describes people as sitting on a 'mountain of gold' and how we need to 'tap into the gold they are sitting on'.

Exnovation is the attempt to improve practices on the basis of what is already present, bringing to the foreground the things hidden in the everyday activity.

Mesman 2016

Videoing provides an extra pair of eyes and a window into the practices and culture of the team or unit. Mesman suggests it provides a way to get an outsider's perspective (a fresh set of eyes provided by the video) balanced with an insider's perspective (the eyes of the people who are used to working with what they have). The video does this by showing people what they do and challenges them to think about what they do and what they then see that they actually do. This opens up 'their mundane', helps them see the things they do every day, the work-as-done. It is not about demonstrating best practice or even simulating a practice or event. It is simply about showing the reality of the actual work and things the people do in a particular environment.

The videoing is either done by the researcher or the staff. The staff's actions are filmed at work, then the footage is analysed and used to reflect as a team in a group meeting. The filming triggers a conversation.

The conversation requires careful facilitation, it requires openness, humility and people seeking to understand rather than judge. During the reflection people are asked to use a form of appreciative inquiry and ask 'what is going well', 'what is going right', 'what are the ingredients of what we are doing well'? Mesman believes that video also promotes collaboration, engagement and experiential learning, especially if it is locally owned and self-managed.

Mesman says that exnovation will not show you everything. No research practice can do that. It is about seeing things differently. It is another method to add to other ways in which we collect information about what we do. Essentially, this is a lovely way of helping people talk to each other about their strengths and what they do well and what they can tweak in order to do it even better. It is less threatening because the premise is to look at things going well.

It sounds like a great way for teams to study how they work and how they work with each other. In order to implement this method it does require time, motivation, resources and obviously permission from staff, patients, families and the leadership of the organisation. The necessary legal and ethical approval must be sought. You can encourage people to give it a go by sharing stories of how useful it has been, what other teams have done and what they have learned.

Another interesting aspect is that it is also a wonderful way that people can see what other people do in relation to the same things that they do. We rarely get to see what other people do in relation to the same tasks we are required to do, for example the way we communicate such as the delivery of bad news or the way we practice such as feeding neonates via a nasogastric tube.

It is often only in training do you get to shadow or observe what other people do, but when you are qualified and in fact the more senior you become, it is rare that you get to observe what other people do.

2.4.4 *Golden Days and Lives Saved*

This is the study of days that go well. Certain criteria are used to decide what a good day looks like; a day when people were kept safe, when teams worked well together, when everything felt like it all went to plan, anything unexpected was managed and so on. Then this is simply recorded on a chart or white board or even an app. Over time the data will show the number of days when all felt good versus the days when it didn't. The next step beyond this would be to take one of those days, bring people together who were there on that day and facilitate a conversation that starts to detect what factors helped make it a good day. Talking about what is working well changes the whole conversation completely. The review does not have to wait for something bad to happen before things are studied and is so much more uplifting to study. There is also an absence of the usual fear associated with an incident or error. If we are able to study our work in this way we will start to have a method for removing blame from failure and error.

A form of this was described to me in February 2019 by a paediatrician who used a method called 'lives saved'. This comes from the Royal National Lifeboat Institution (RNLI) which makes a distinction between people aided and lives saved. In the UK there were around 170 drownings and coastal fatalities in 2013. The RNLI aims to prevent more tragedies through their rescue operations. They assess each rescue operation and if they consider that if they had not been there or if they had not intervened the person or persons would have died then they call that a 'life saved'. This is then added to a board at the lifeboat base and the numbers are used to assess each year how many lives the RNLI saved. The paediatrician I mentioned previously has decided that for every patient they believe would have died if it had not been for their care or intervention then they register that as a 'life saved'. This has led to their ability to collect the number of lives saved in their area. He cited how uplifting this was and how positive it was for staff who are quoted as going home at the end of a shift and telling their family and friends 'I saved a life today'.

The joy of this is that it is simply a tool to lift morale. We don't have to get hung up on subjective definitions of a life saved; this is not a research study. It is simply a way of reminding people that what they do matters, that what they do does save people's lives. It could also be used as a way of asking some key questions about the care and what was it that was so successful that day.

2.5 Functional Resonance Analysis Method

As discussed earlier, the underlying models for understanding accidents and incidents have been criticised as being too simplistic or too linear for capturing the multiple parallel factors that contribute to incidents (Hollnagel 2012b, Furniss et al. 2019). This has led to the introduction of methods to try to capture these systemic complexities, one being the Functional Resonance Analysis Method (FRAM) (Hollnagel 2012b and 2014).

2.5.1 What Is the Functional Resonance Analysis Method or FRAM?

FRAM is a relatively new method proposed by Hollnagel (2012 and 2014) to carry out either a retrospective analysis to explain a specific incident or prospectively to analyse processes to identify potential risks and conditions that may impact on safety. This method has gained a lot of traction within healthcare safety as it can explore functional variability and how this can escalate into unexpected and often unwanted events (Furniss et al. 2019). It has mainly been used to study things that have gone wrong but increasingly is being applied to areas that succeed (Furniss et al. 2019, Hollnagel 2014). It has gradually been realised that it is a mistake to work with one type of explanations for actions that go well and another for actions that go badly (Hollnagel 2014).

FRAM is both about studying and measuring work-as-done in order to strengthen what works but also to see how we can measure and strengthen the reliability of the system. This method has been found to be useful in illustrating complexity and the aspects of complexity (as described earlier) which include the relationships, the dynamics and the huge number of interactions even in the simplest of tasks.

FRAM is an analysis tool that reflects both resilience engineering and 'Ssafety II' thinking. It helps people who work in safety understand why and how people might 'work round' what is needed or should be done, which steps they always do and which ones they might miss. For example, they may not wash their hands prior to the resuscitation of a patient who has collapsed because they need to carry out the task very quickly and there are no facilities to wash their hands in close proximity. There are often many possibilities to consider. In fact, the combination of different inputs, outputs, resources and so on in healthcare are almost always unique every single time so every interaction with every different patient becomes something people have never done before. This is the way in which we do things in healthcare, learn from different cases and patients in order to help with decision making for future patients while at all times recognising that the actions and decisions will be unique to each patient.

What FRAM does is demonstrate how the study of the combination of people with the processes, guidance, resources and conditions can be used to help strengthen the safety of healthcare. It opens up a set of questions in relation to variability, violations, interdependence and complexity that may help people optimise the work they do.

The combined performance variability of everyone in the system is not particularly noticed (unless it goes wrong) and is considered 'random noise'. However, Hollnagel (2012) asserts that variability is not as random as it may seem to be. The variability is in the main due to the adjustments of people individually and collectively. These adjustments are purposive and recognisable by those doing them as they are often regular workarounds or shortcuts. There can, in fact, be a regularity in the way that people respond to the unexpected situations that arise.

A resilient system can mean that people respond to what the system and others do but also to what they expect the system and others to do; they anticipate what may happen and take action accordingly. This then gives rise to the dependencies of the actions of the different individuals and the system. Hollnagel (2014) describes these as 'mutual approximate adjustments'. Functional resonance is proposed by Hollnagel as a way to understand outcomes that are both non-causal (emergent) and non-linear in a way that makes both potentially predicable and controllable.

2.5.2 Terminology

First, we need to consider the terms used.

A function is defined as something a system does or the means that are necessary to achieve a goal (Hollnagel 2012b). It represents all of the acts or activities (simple and complicated and complex) that are needed to produce a result. A function typically describes what people individually or collectively have to do to perform a specific task and thus achieve a specific goal, for example triage a patient or carry out medication reconciliation or administer a nasogastric feed.

A function can refer to something an organisation does – for example the function of an emergency department is to treat incoming patients or of a general practice is to diagnose, treat or reassure patients within their clinic. A function can also refer to a technical system such as a dialysis machine or a ventilator, in both how it functions on its own and how it functions with other technical systems and the people operating them.

Each function has six different 'aspects' that shape how functions can be related or coupled when using this method, i.e., the output of one function might impact the resources or be a precondition of another (Hollnagel 2012):

- Input (I): that which the function processes or transforms or that which starts the function.
- Output (O): that which is the result of the function, either an entity or a state change.
- Preconditions (P): conditions that must exist before a function can be carried out.
- Resources (R): that which the function needs when it is carried out (Execution Condition) or consumes to produce the Output.
- Time (T): time-based constraints affecting the function (with regard to starting time, finishing time and duration).
- Control (C): how the function is monitored or controlled.

These aspects will start to define the potential variability of the function and how functions are related.

What follows is a medication example (Hollnagel 2014 p.24):

> The pharmacy has an assistant, who oversees the supply of medications. Medications are delivered to the pharmacy section in sealed boxes, a delivery confirmation is signed, and the sealed boxes are placed in a locked medication room. When the medication is prepared for a specific patient, it is placed in a pill container with a patient ID label attached. Before the medication is administered, the label is

scanned to make sure it is for the correct patient. In order to receive their medication, patients go to, but do not enter, the medication room. The Clerk makes sure all patients receive their medication. The Nurse actually administers the medication. If the Nurse leaves the medication room to take care of a patient during the process, the door to the medication room must be closed and locked.

After finding the tasks, we can describe them as activities (using verbs).

- Oversee the supply of medications.
- Deliver medications.
- Acknowledge (or sign) the delivery of medication.
- Place the medications in the room.
- Attach a label to the pill container.
- Place medication in a patient-specific pill container with a label attached.
- Scan label to confirm the right medication is given to the right patient.
- Make sure all patients get medication.
- Administer the medication to each patient.
- Discontinue medication administration temporarily to attend to other jobs.
- Close door.
- Lock door.

These twelve functions can be used as a basis for describing how the work is done in practice. This description may in turn be used to analyse a specific pathway or event. This is done by describing each function in detail, including who performs it and as many of the six aspects (Input, Output, Requirements, Resources, Control and Time) that are relevant to understanding how the function can be performed.

Central to FRAM is the idea of resonance. This is described by Hollnagel and his colleagues in what follows (2014 p.20).

> The variability of a number of functions may some-times coincide, i.e., they may mutually influence each other. This can cause the amplitude of one or more functions to become unusually large (leading to either positive or negative outcomes). The consequences of such increased variability may spread to other functions in analogy with the phenomenon of resonance. It is thus no longer a question of single or multiple cause-effect chains, because that would imply that one could speak of one or more specific and recognisable causes (something that went wrong). The impacts instead emerge, i.e., they appear in a manner that can-not be explained by or reduced to linear causality.
>
> There are three types of resonance. In physi-cal systems, classical resonance is the phenomenon that a system can oscillate with larger amplitude at some frequencies than at others. These are known as the system's resonant (or resonance) frequencies. At these frequencies even small external forces that are applied repeatedly can produce large amplitude oscillations, which may seriously damage or even destroy the system. Classical resonance has been known at least since ancient Greece. A more recent form is stochastic resonance, has been understood since the early 1980s. In stochastic resonance there is no forcing function, but rather random noise, which every now and then pushes a subliminal signal over the detection threshold. Stochastic resonance can be defined as the enhanced sensitivity of a device to a weak signal that occurs when random noise is added to the mix. The outcome of stochastic resonance is non-linear, which simply means that the output is not directly proportional to the input. The outcome can

also occur instantaneously, unlike classical resonance which must be built-up over time.

A third type of resonance, which is central to the FRAM, is called functional resonance. As a phenomenon, functional resonance describes the noticeable performance variability in a socio-technical system that is the outcome of the multiple approximate adjustments that are the basis for everyday work activities. Functional resonance is the detectable outcome (or signal) that emerges from the unintended interaction of the everyday variability of multiple signals. The approximate adjustments comprise a small number of recognisable short-cuts or heuristics, which means that performance variability is semi-orderly and therefore also partly predictable. There is a regularity in how people behave and in how they respond to unexpected situations – including those that arise from how other people behave. The resonance effects that occur can be seen as a consequence of the ways in which the system functions, and the phenomenon is therefore called functional resonance rather than stochastic resonance. Functional resonance offers a way to understand outcomes that are both non-causal (emergent) and non-linear (disproportionate) in a way that makes both predictability and control possible.

Functional resonance is defined as 'the detectable signal that emerges from the unintended interaction of the everyday variability of multiple signals' (Hollnagel 2012 p.67).

2.5.3 The Four Steps

Hollnagel proposes the following four steps:

1. Identify and describe the important system functions that are required for everyday work to succeed – characterise each function using the six basic characteristics (IOPRTC seen earlier).

2. Characterise the potential variability of these functions as well as the possible actual variability of the functions in one or more implementations of the model.
3. Determine the possibility of functional resonance based on the dependencies or couplings among functions. That is, understand how the variability of the functions may have combined and then determine whether this led to the unexpected outcomes.
4. Develop recommendations for the way forward on how to monitor and influence the variability either by limiting the variability that can lead to undesirable results or by enhancing the variability that can lead to desired results.

What follows is a resuscitation example:

■ First step is to think about the important system functions for resuscitation; the processes, the inputs, the outputs, the preconditions, resources (staffing, equipment, and time), the skills and knowledge required and so on. For example, oxygen, drugs, flat surface, people, knowledge on how to do mouth to mouth, training, knowledge on how to do compressions, a defibrillator, an intensive care, someone to transport the patient and so on.

■ Second step is to describe the potential variables and actual variables associated with resuscitation. For example, we know that resuscitation is different depending upon the care setting and environment. There is potentially a range of ways in which a patient could be resuscitated depending upon where they collapsed. There are different techniques for a person who has collapsed and is lying on a soft surface versus a hard surface, collapsed on the floor versus a bed or collapsed in a confined space like a toilet versus the open ward or clinic. In hospital there is a vast array of tools and components that can support the resuscitation of a patient, far less so in the community and almost none if someone collapses in the middle of a park. So by describing the multiple potential and actual variants of resuscitation depending upon the people, skills, resources and environment it helps understand the variability of performance that is necessary to carry out the function.

■ Thirdly we can then understand how the variability (or variables) associated with what should happen and what did happen and how these variables may have combined and work out how they have helped people carry out a good resuscitation or whether these variables hindered people's abilities which led to a poor outcome. All of this information can also be matched to what we may know already; information or cases when patients were unsuccessfully and successfully resuscitated. The fourth step is to propose recommendations for replicating, optimising and strengthening' doing things differently in order for the outcome to be more successful in the future.

2.5.4 The Four Principles

The four principles on which the FRAM is built are:

1. Failures and successes *are equivalent* in the sense that they have the same origin; that things go right and go wrong for the same reasons.
2. The everyday performance of socio-technical systems, including humans individually and collectively, is always *adjusted* to match the conditions.
3. Many of the outcomes we notice, as well as many that we do not, must be described as *emergent* i.e., that they evolve and arise out of a failure or success rather than being as resultant or a consequence of the failure or success.
4. That the relations and dependencies among the functions of a system must be described each time as they develop in a specific situation rather than as predetermined cause and effect links and this is done by 'functional resonance'.

To expand this further:

Equivalence of failures and successes: This as we have seen is the concept of 'Safety II' and the view that failure and success flow from the same sources. The fact that decisions made today may lead to success and the exact same decisions tomorrow may lead to failure depending upon the different circumstances and conditions that are faced when those decisions are made resonates strongly with those that work in healthcare.

Adjustments: We have seen how as healthcare professionals we constantly adapt and adjust our performance to keep things going, to keep our patients safe. We are masters at creating order out of disorder and making sense out of confusing situations. This is the messy reality of healthcare. This is how we work. In these circumstances human performance will always be variable. In healthcare it is more than simply working out how people perform. It is understanding their ability to perform under extreme conditions, while they are chronically fatigued and stressed, being constantly interrupted and distracted, running up and down floors to find where their patients are or where the nearest telephone is or where they can go to the toilet. Then imagine coping with the heat, noise and crumbling buildings of most healthcare settings. People adjust what they do to match the conditions. People are the reason why things go right far more often than they go wrong. Adjustments, therefore, can be argued to be a strength rather than a liability. Healthcare professionals are extremely adept at finding ways of overcoming the problems at work and this capability is vital for safety.

Emergence: When something happens in healthcare an explanation is sought and the model of causality is applied. Hollnagel believes that this should be described as emergent (Hollnagel 2012).

Resonance: FRAM is mainly used to focus on monitoring functional resonance that amplifies uncontrolled performance variability to cause unexpected and unwanted outcomes. Furniss and colleagues (2019) have changed the focus to positive resonance that amplifies the effectiveness of processes and the potential for successful outcomes.

2.5.5 Examples of Questions

When do you start this activity?

What 'signals' that you can begin?

How do you adjust the activity to different conditions?

How do you determine how and when to adjust?

How do you respond if something unexpected happens? For example, an interruption, a pause required by a more urgent task that takes priority, a missing resource, etc.

How stable is staffing?

Is staff allocation permanently assigned or adjusted daily?

What happens if staffing is short?

How stable is the environment? Supplies? Resources? Demands?

Are there often undesirable conditions that you have to tolerate or get used to?

What preconditions are usually met?

Are there factors that are taken for granted?

How do you prepare for your work (documents, instructions, colleagues)?

What do you do if these resources are not available?

What information do you need (equipment, services)?

What do you do if this is not available?

How does time pressure affect your work?

What skills do you need?

Does everyone performing this work have these skills?

What is the optimal way to perform this work?

Is there an optimal way?

How often do you change or adjust your work?

2.5.6 FRAM and Safety

FRAM is used to describe the functions that are required for the system to achieve its purpose. But because they will be different every time there is a further layer of information which is to describe the potential performance variability of these functions. This will also pick up how the variables can be combined in unexpected or unintended ways.

The dilemma facing those that work in safety is that the situation or system is rarely improved by eliminating performance variability since it is essential to ensure safety. The solution is instead to manage performance variability by trying to minimise its effects. How many times have we heard 'we need to learn lessons so that the same thing doesn't happen again to someone else'? It feels like a mantra we have been using for years and years. The solutions we should all be seeking are to replicate good practice, optimise performance and strengthen systems rather than to eliminate hazards or even to prevent hazards by using barriers which may in fact hinder.

There are many different methods for event analysis and risk assessment and FRAM is just one of these. However, while the use of FRAM is in its infancy in healthcare there appears to be an appetite for an alternative model that brings together the different concepts of resilience engineering, 'Safety II' and complexity, so that we can understand the system functions better and the performance variability in so much more detail that we do presently. It may also help us to move away from looking at one incident at a time and looking at the functions of a system as a way to prevent the single incidents from happening. The analysis of a past or future event uses a FRAM model to understand how something happened (an event), to assess how something may happen (a risk analysis), or to assess the impact of changes and improvements (design). The FRAM can therefore be used as part of event analysis, as part of risk assessment, or as part of the design process, but is strictly speaking neither an accident analysis method, a risk assessment method, nor a design method (Hollnagel 2014 p.60).

> The purpose of this model is to make sure that performance variability is understood and managed rather than just preventing the specific event from happening again. If we can understand the performance variability we may not only prevent the specific event from happening again but many more.

2.6 Measurement and Monitoring Framework

> We should not try to measure safety at all – instead we should seek to understand every day work, find some things you would like to keep track of and notice what is happening – the combination of small things and behaviours and systems that are constantly changing.
>
> **Hollnagel 2016**

This feels like quite a challenge being set by Hollnagel. It sometimes feels impossible to measure safety or the absence of harm or whether a system is safer today than it was yesterday. It feels like the measures are blunt and clumsy and making things possibly worse than 'trying not to measure safety at all' seems the right thing to do. However, this has not stopped people from trying.

> Measurement is always wrong though sometimes useful.
>
> **Berwick 2019**

In metrics, there are errors and loss of meaning and they create an imperfect construct of reality. Measures can be turned into a game and can be manipulated. This in turn can change what we do which is not always helpful. It shifts the purpose towards meeting the needs of the measures. Measurement always produces misunderstanding unless it is supported by conversation. There is a psychology of measurement. How it affects us depends on why we are measuring, for example if it is in in the spirit of inspection or for learning Berwick (2019) says:

■ Never confuse metrics with what is important.
■ Use conversation if you can.
■ Learn about the best way to measure and do not rely on only red, yellow and green lights.
■ Remember that graphs tell stories.
■ Stop measuring things that are not needed – decide when enough is enough.

At the same time as the concepts of 'Safety I' and 'Safety II' were emerging Vincent, Burnett and Carthey developed a framework for measuring and monitoring safety (Vincent et al. 2013, 2014). The authors agreed that there was a struggle in healthcare to understand whether to focus on error, harm or reliability or the positive face of safety. At the time of their study there was no clear framework for organising our thinking or our measurement strategy for safety. They found that safety was a very confusing topic for many people and that the measurement and monitoring of safety was often narrowly focused (Vincent et al. 2013). The measurement and monitoring framework was therefore developed to help provide a way in which safety could and should be measured. However it is so much more than that. It is about so much more than measurement, as another expert on patient safety implementation Garrett, who teaches internationally on the measurement and monitoring framework, says:

The framework really expands our view of safety, moving us beyond the 'rear view mirror' of harm that has already occurred, towards focusing on how to proactively manage risk and create safety. It also highlights the importance of paying attention to 'soft intelligence' – gained from observation, intuition, listening, and talking with staff, patients and families – as well using hard data and metrics. This helps us shift from our current emphasis on assurance to one of inquiry and deeper understanding. The framework may look simple, but that's deceptive. Understood properly, it fundamentally challenges the way we traditionally think about safety and what we need to do to measure and improve it.

Garrett 2019

In line with their resilience engineering colleagues the authors felt that measuring safety should not be solely about measuring harm and that looking at safety retrospectively was not a reliable indicator of whether the organisation or unit or practice was 'safe' now or whether it would be 'safe' in the future. They share the view with Hollnagel (2013) that 'safety is a dynamic non-event'.

Vincent and his colleagues (2013) build on the debate about what patient safety is or isn't. In many people's view, patient safety is equated to learning about harm, capturing incidents and doing investigations and that it is focused solely on error. This still remains the case today and is limiting our efforts to make care safer. As the authors rightly say 'harm is what patients care most about'. But if we focus purely on harm and error then we are not really learning about how the system is functioning. For example, if the harm is presumed to arise mostly from error then what of the times when harm has not occurred due to error or the errors that do not lead to harm.

Monitoring is all about understanding where you are in relation to where you want to be and it is not always about the statistics or the numbers. It can be a feeling. We can use the models described in the previous section to construct questions that can be used to understand how well the organisation is performing and use these questions to engage frontline workers. Knowing where you are now can help with anticipation about what could, should or might happen from here. What needs to happen to reach our goals, what things need to happen, are we on track or not? It helps build a shared understanding between staff and between staff and patients. Measurement needs a purpose; to learn and to look at changes while at the same time not to worry about the actual position.

> We measure everything at work except what counts
>
> **Heffernan 2015**

2.6.1 The Five Dimensions

The framework describes five dimensions which the authors believe should be included in all aspects of safety and monitoring in healthcare. By doing so the organisation will have a much more rounded picture of their organisation's safety. These five dimensions are:

1. Past harm: both psychological and physical measures.
2. Reliability: building a 'failure free operation over time'. This is about measuring behaviour, processes and systems.
3. Sensitivity to operations: the information needed and the capacity to monitor safety on a day-to-day basis.
4. Anticipation and preparedness: the ability to anticipate and be prepared for things that may go wrong.
5. Integration and learning: the ability to respond to and improve from safety information.

The report and the framework offer people at all levels of healthcare organisations and the wider system some great insights into what they need to think about and do to move away from the current retrospective and reactive mode. It shifts them to think more prospectively and proactively. This is because the framework focuses on leading indicators rather than just lagging, shifting to proactive management and creation of safety (i.e., not seeing this as just absence of harm), looking at work-as-done rather than work-as-imagined, shifting from assurance, reassurance and compliance to enquiry and learning. The framework pays as much attention to monitoring and 'soft intelligence' including observation, listening, feeling and intuition, conversations with patients, families and staff, as measurement, as it does to hard data and numbers.

2.6.2 *The Five Questions*

The five questions that the framework suggests can help enhance 'Safety I' and support 'Safety II' are:

Has patient care been safe in the past? Study data associated with past harm but also design more nuanced measures of harm that can be tracked over time and can clearly demonstrate that healthcare is becoming safer.

Are our clinical systems and processes reliable? Use the three models set out by Vincent and Amalberti together with Amalberti's dynamic systems model to understand how the system works every single time and what happens when it doesn't. The key issue is how can the basic reliability of healthcare be measured and monitored. It is particularly hard because staff may not realise that they are being unreliable and they may have accepted poor reliability as their 'normal'. There is a lack of feedback from the system to tell the workers that they are being safe or unsafe and in many cases a lack of standardisation for people to be able to compare actual (work-as-done) care versus the standard (work-as-prescribed). The only clear way to measure this is set out a number of processes that are expected to be as reliable as they can be across the whole system. Then to have a baseline of data for these processes and then capture data over time to compare with the baseline. Find some simple measures, such as documentation of allergy status which we know should be done for all patients.

Is care safety today? This is described as 'sensitivity to operations' which is a term used by high-reliability theorists. It includes awareness of all the conditions, pressures, circumstances that can impact on patient care every day (work-as-done). It is suggested that huddles, briefings and de-briefings and interviews of staff and patients can be used to understand this.

Will care be safe in the future? This is about anticipation and preparedness and trying to predict what may happen in the future. Risk assessment and risk registers have been traditionally used for this. Other models include human reliability analysis and failure modes and effects analysis – two methods for systematically plotting and examining a process and the ways in which it may fail. However, in my experience, these are rarely understood or used in healthcare.

Are we responding and improving? This is about the learning part of measurement and monitoring. As has been set out in the section on safety myths, learning from incident reporting and incident investigation is patchy.

2.7 Change the Language to Change the Mindset

The final section of Part Two is all about the words we use. They really matter. Our language affects the way we view the world and our words have consequences. Language emerges from the way in which we interact with each other, and it changes all of the time. It includes slang, jargon and dialect divergence and there can be different meanings for the same word depending upon the cultural influence.

Language is pivotal to shifting the culture of safety. Consider the language you use and whether it promotes a safe culture or perpetuates the blame culture – consider the language that opens people up or shuts them down. What we have learned is the importance of using the right language to talk about safety. Words like kindness, gratitude, joy and respect are not words usually associated with safety. However, these beautiful words connect with the real emotions of people and are needed to build a safety culture which is usually filled with words like clinical negligence, assurance, governance, incident reporting, patient safety, clinical risk, resilience, high reliability and quality improvement. Most of the time the language of safety has negative connotations such as human error, legal battles, blunders, violations, mistakes, failure and never events.

> If we wish to change the mindset of how we can make healthcare safer we need to enrich our language with positive words; adjustments, adaptation, working safely, positive deviance, kindness, gratitude, success and optimisation and use these in preference to the current negative labels.

The language that we use in safety is subtle but powerful in terms of how it impacts on what and how people feel. If people are encouraged to frame things in a caring and compassionate way then they in turn may be more caring and compassionate. If we start by asking positive questions; What are you proud of? What brings joy to your work? What do you get right? Was everything as safe as you would like it to be?' This depersonalises it and enables people to say how they would like things to be which in turn is describing when it isn't. If we ask these questions before we ask 'what went wrong' then it shifts the way in which we look at safety. If we use even simple words like 'what' rather than 'who' it shifts the focus from the person to the system.

'Safety II' helps us to talk about what works rather than what goes wrong and in turn it changes the tone and language of the conversation completely. It is morale boosting and brings people together. Use the words 'restorative just culture' which means we are much more positive about people's actions and behaviours because people are seen as the solution rather than the problem. This creates a more positive, inclusive and more effective learning environment for improving patient safety.

Traditional term	Proposed term
Patient safety: this term puts safety in a box, or a role or a session at a workshop. It becomes the responsibility of the 'head of patient safety' and the 'patient safety team'	Working safely: takes it from one person's responsibility to belonging to everyone
Human error: focuses on the human as the lead cause for error	Performance variability: helps us consider the people and the system together
Zero harm: an impossibility – sets people up to fail and leads to fear of disclosure	Natural variation: makes it clear that we can never have a perfectly safe system and that people will make mistakes
Improvement: assumes that something needs improving when it could be working adequately	Strengthen: shifts us to look to strengthen and optimise what works
Violations: assumes that everyone who does not follow a policy is 'violating' the policy (in the wrong way)	Adjustments: assumes that people adjust and adapt what they do to do their very best for their patients

2.7.1 Patient Safety

Hollnagel challenges us to think about our definitions and language when talking about 'safety', that we should move away from these titles or easily boxed-in headings (such as patient safety) to talking more widely about 'working safely' (Hollnagel 2013).

Helping people 'work safely' moves things from being owned by an individual or a team to something everyone should do.

It moves patient safety from a workshop or a strategy to about everything we do, every action we take and every decision we make. Patient safety should be redefined as working safely and should be defined as:

working safely (in relation to patient care) is ensuring that that the number of intended and acceptable outcomes is as high as possible and people are supported to adjust what they do to match the conditions of actual work, that we learn to identify and overcome the flaws in the system, and interpret and apply policies and procedures to match those conditions

2.7.2 Human Error

The words 'human error' make a particular judgement. Human error clearly sets out that it is the human who is the cause of the problem and is responsible for the outcome. In the main people use the term 'with good intent' to help people understand that human error is normal i.e., 'we all make mistakes'. But it implies that any failure, causal or contributory, is the fault of the human. In theory the term human error relates to how human performance of a specific function might fail to reach its objectives rather than whether the human failed but in practice the term misleads people to focus on the error of the human. It implies that humans can be also fixed in some way; that the error is in some way controllable or a choice. It points to the individual rather than the system in which they work. By simplifying this to being a cause then the solution to this is to stop the human from making the errors either by stopping them continuing or to restrict them in some way. However, we know that incorrect human actions at the frontline are due to a deeper set of symptoms within the system or the workplace.

Human error also stigmatises actions that could have been the right actions in slightly different circumstances.

There is a fine line between the right and wrong actions which is often only determined when there is an end result or a known outcome. Human error is too often used to describe carelessness, laziness or incompetence and is highly subject to outcome bias. What if we don't use the term human error at all? Preferred terms are error on its own or performance variability, or erroneous conditions or system error. If all 'human activity is variable in that it is adjusted to the conditions' then the variability is a strength, indeed it is a necessity rather than a liability. As many say, failure is the flip side of success. By acknowledging that 'performance always varies and never is flawless, the need of a separate category for human error evaporates' (Hollnagel 2016).

2.7.3 Honest Mistake

I frequently hear people talk about how there should be a 'no blame' culture for people who commit an honest mistake. When does a mistake stop being honest? How can a mistake be dishonest? The language implies a judgement associated with the natural things we do as human beings.

2.7.4 Violations

In 'Safety I' the bad outcome is often attributed to the behaviour of the frontline staff. If they have been found to not comply with a rule or guideline or policy then they are judged to have 'violated' that prescribed form of work. These are referred to in the safety world as 'violations'. People who commit violations are considered risky or reckless in their behaviour and are often threatened with sanctions. This adds to the fear of disclosing what actually happens in the everyday work, the workarounds they do, the guidance they don't follow. This fear silences people and they may either keep quiet or lie. This may lead to what people describe as the work-as-disclosed i.e., that people will only disclose what they think other people want to hear.

Violations are said to occur when healthcare practitioners are faced with situations in which they may need to take a risk. These are often referred to as violations because individuals or groups take action which is different from the expected standard or rules or procedures i.e., they violated the policy. Much can be learned by understanding why certain violations happen and why some become the norm. So the response required is to pause before judging and to try to understand why. Catchpole (2013) states; 'violations and non-adherence are common, not always conscious, not always planned, are frequently well meaning, and in many cases allow the system to run smoothly'. Understanding why people 'violate' policies and procedures is a key component of patient safety. The reasons may lead to valuable lessons for the organisation who may need to rewrite some of the standards or rules or may have to consider how these rules could be made easier to implement. Simplistic labels like violations are symptoms of a simplistic approach to safety. They are usually only applied to frontline decisions rather than those made at the 'blunt end' of the organisation, such as by the senior leaders and board.

There are a number of different types of violations:

- Erroneous – the clinician did not fully understand the policy and was not aware of the right steps to make.
- Routine – it is routine to move patients around the hospital when other parts are full or busy.
- Situational or exceptional – the clinician changes the normal procedure for a patient.
- Optimising – it appeared to be better to do the procedure in a different way.
- Unintentional – the clinician did not intend to do the wrong thing.

The words violating or violation have very strong connotations of 'disgraceful behaviour'; the tone is already set for those who are found to have not adhered to a set procedure for some reason or other. We don't have a clear understanding of the scale and nature of the problem of violations. They are usually related to 'work-as-done', they become normal, the 'way we do things round here'. If regarded as usual practice (not necessarily the written practice) then they can only be detected when something goes wrong. Violations should instead be termed as adjustments or adaptations.

2.7.5 Zero Harm

Another term that needs consideration is 'zero harm' and it's friend 'never events'. Zero harm is impossible. There is a belief that if we count all the failures and we find all the causes of those failures and treat them that accidents and incidents are therefore preventable, this he termed the 'zero harm principle'.

> Zero harm is a very attractive goal for many but not realistic
>
> **Hollnagel 2016**

Improvers like to use 'stretch goals' and in this respect they would probably say that aiming for zero harm is a stretch goal and that there is nothing wrong with having this dream or aspiration. But we have to accept that a system can never be 'safe', it can only be as safe as possible. Healthcare is never about certainty; it is about the balance of probabilities and risk. It is filled with people who will make mistakes no matter how hard they try to be perfect. They are often working in systems that are not well designed or not designed to help people work safely and in conditions that increase the chances of things going wrong. If we tell them that we should aim for zero harm then every time things don't go as planned then they will feel like they are letting everyone down and that they have failed within an expectation that they should be perfect.

We must not perpetuate the myth of zero harm because it assumes that all accidents or incidents have causes and if they can be identified it should therefore follow that they can be prevented and therefore they can be reduced to zero. This is an impossibility.

2.7.6 *Never Events*

Never events make safety language even more negative. Never events, is a similar term to zero harm in that it is a term used for a subset of incidents that are deemed preventable. They are defined as 'serious incidents that are wholly preventable, as guidance or safety recommendations that provide strong systemic protective barriers are available at a national level and should have been implemented by all healthcare providers'. In the English healthcare system, there is a list of never events. Once the type of harm is described as a never event, then the goal is for the harm to never happen but because of the inevitability of error in complex adaptive systems they will happen. So what happens is the leaders of organisations and frontline staff are then blamed when they do. This means that they are so fearful of reporting never events that they distort reporting and encourage under-reporting of a never event. No one wants them to happen but they do. If they are used to judge individuals, teams or organisations then the people will do their best to hide them. The opposite of never is ever or always and that in itself is as unachievable as never. So perhaps instead of the words never event or zero harm we should focus on language that is achievable or possible or attainable.

2.8 Part Two Summary

Part Two describes the combination of a different mindset, a different language, a different way of implementing the concepts and models. We have explored how safety can be improved by studying everyday situations where safety is present and how that in order to do this we need to help people narrow the gap between work-as-done and work-as-imagined and we need to help people succeed under the varying conditions. There are four 'works' that help us think about how people can work safely:

■ Work-as-done
■ Work-as-imagined
■ Work-as-prescribed
■ Work-as-disclosed

There are a number of methods or models that can help people to work safely:.

■ Ethnography and simulation
■ Positive deviance
■ Exnovation
■ Golden days and lives saved
■ Functional Resonance Analysis Method (FRAM)

All of these methods or models help safety professionals and others study what happens all of the time by simply observing day-to-day practice in a particular area. They are useful to aiding the study of established practices and to paying attention to the mundane, to the implicit local routines, to what is in place. They help looks at the variations in performance and processes that result in good outcomes rather than poor outcomes or harm. Their purpose is to understand performance variability and manage it in two different ways (enhancing the variability that leads to success and decreasing the variability that leads to failure) rather than just preventing a specific event or incident from happening again. If we can understand the performance variability we may not only prevent the specific event from happening again but many more.

The latest thinking challenges us to think about how we measure and monitor safety with a practical framework which also brings to life the concepts of 'Safety II' and complexity. We are also challenged to consider our definitions and language when talking about safety and patient safety, human error, violations and zero harm. We should move away from these titles or easily boxed-in headings to talking more widely about how we can help both people and systems to work safely'acknowledging that there will be adjustments made and that we can never make the healthcare system entirely free from failure or harm.

2.9 Part Two Actions

What follows are a few actions for turning the theory into practice.

- Understand the difference between work-as-done and work-as-imagined.
- Understand the challenges of work-as-prescribed and work-as-disclosed.
- Build cultures that support people to disclose and to tell the truth – seek to learn rather than judge.
- Find out what the myths and rules are and dispel the myths and help with the rules to make things easy.
- Find the experts in your areas who really know their areas well.
- Be humble and be curious and at all times seek to learn and not to judge.
- Test out the models to understand work-as-done to find out what adjustments people are making every day, what workarounds they may be doing in order to keep things going – find out the lived reality of the people and teams in your organisation.
- Design systems that help people make adjustments safely.
- Use the principles of 'Safety II' in all improvement work.
- Integrate all of these principles into your safety strategies including your incident reporting and investigation frameworks.

- If you are designing an intervention, guideline or strategy start by understanding how work is done and not how you imagine it to be.
- Never issue a policy or a guideline that has not been through the process of ensuring that it fits the reality of where it is going to land.
- Every policy in healthcare should carry the following message 'and we might adjust and adapt this in light of the circumstances'.
- Use the FRAM model to study performance variability rather than simply looking at individual incidents to prevent them from happening again. If we can understand the performance variability we may not only prevent the specific event from happening again but many more. Test out the four steps:
  1. Identify the functions that are required for everyday work to succeed by describing how something is done in detail.
  2. Characterise the variability of these functions including both the potential variability of the functions and the expected actual variability in the incident.
  3. Look at the specific incident and understand how the variability of the functions may have combined and determine whether this led to unexpected outcomes.
  4. Propose ways to manage the possible occurrences of uncontrolled performance variability found in steps one to three.
- Consider your language in all your internal and external communications – make it positive and remove any undertones of blaming language. Exchange terms like patient safety with working safely, human error with erroneous conditions or performance variability, and violations with adjustments.
- Talk to you staff about helping them work safely rather than 'doing patient safety'.

- Accept that zero harm is not possible and don't set your staff up to fail by expecting that they can be perfect.
- Balance the two lexicons in public policy
  - The language of metrics, productivity, cost savings, value adding and regulation (rational) – evidence-based and measurable (which may ignore what really matters to people)
  - The language of kindness, empathy, joy, gratitude, love and friendship (relational) – to encourage a warmth and responsiveness that humans need.

Part Three

Urgently Tackle the Culture of Blame

Because healthcare's complicated, it's a DIFFICULT WORK ENVIRONMENT.

Pressures, unhelpful cultures, stress, incivility and bulltying, make it harder to WORK SAFELY.

3.1 Part Three Introduction

In Parts One and Two we have seen how most people make countless adjustments during their work. The vast majority of these lead to success; a small minority lead to failure. This is just how we work. We have to take the blame out of failure, which leads me to Part Three and how we have to urgently tackle the culture of blame in healthcare.

I have had the privilege of talking to many people who work in healthcare and in one of these lectures I spoke to a large number of students, nurses, midwives, paramedics and allied health professionals. I spoke about Safety I and Safety II and the exciting new developments in patient safety. I talked about how we need to consider the conditions in which staff are working and, in particular, the issues of kindness and gratitude. Within this talk I also mentioned the issues highlighted in this section around blame culture and incivility. What surprised and saddened me was that the only thing the students wanted to ask questions about and to discuss further was in relation to blame culture and incivility and its impact on their lives both in the university and in their placements. They talked about how lonely they felt, how isolated they were, how invisible they were made to feel and how rude everyone was to them. They cited the sneers, the belittling and humiliation and the fact that most of the time people could not even be bothered to know their name – simply referring to them as 'the student'.

In healthcare the increase of rudeness and incivility is, in my view, a result of the negative workplaces, negative language, negative relationships and working conditions which include long hours, night shifts, distractions, stress and a variety of pressures. In addition, the language and methods of safety have added to this.

Incivility is a threat to your organisation and the culture within it. However, it is not acknowledged and in many cases people suffer in silence, so it is hidden.

Part Three will explore culture, blame and shame, incivility and bullying as well as the hope that a restorative just culture can bring to us all.

3.2 Culture

The word culture originated from the mid-15th century as directly related to cultivating, caring and tilling the land. In 1867, we see the first use of it in terms of 'collective customs and achievements of a people'. Definitions of culture commonly refer to values, attitudes, norms, beliefs, practices, rules, policies and behaviours of a society, a group of people, a unit or across an organisation. Culture is transmitted through language, material objects, ritual, institutions and art, from one generation to the next. It includes the ideas, customs and social behaviour of a particular people or society, 'the way we do things around here (when people aren't looking)' and the sum of attitudes, customs and beliefs that distinguishes one group of people from another.

Organisational and institutional culture has developed over years, often over decades, and more and the cultures are an accumulation of different experiences, different sets of values and different leadership. It is frequently hard to define and simplistic in its measure and rarely accurately described.

Culture is not a lever. You can't manipulate it. You can't design it. It can be influenced, but it is much easier to influence badly by intervention. Work on the work with the people who do the work and are affected by it ... and culture change comes for free.

Shorrock 2018

3.2.1 Healthcare Culture

Culture in healthcare is characterised by informal systems, workarounds, emergent behaviours and constant adaptations. There are multiple layers and hierarchies, an ecosystem of interacting people, the cliques, the professionals, the informal and formal groups and teams and a variety of different care settings providing or supporting care. There are cultures and subcultures, good and bad relationships, emergent behaviours and politics to contend with. This is combined with multiple objects and functions for people to use and interact with and multifaceted patients, who are monitored, medicated, admitted, treated, moved about and discharged.

Healthcare is filled with a huge variety of people who are at different times motivated and demotivated, or careful, organised and disorganised or making and breaking and following rules. They have different professions, skills, knowledge, status, power and purpose. Healthcare cultures, practices, attitudes and behaviours emerge in unexpected ways, local rules arise and adapt over time and people form into relatively enduring networks, groups and teams.

3.2.2 Safety Culture

We 'must change the safety culture' is a frequent call from investigations and inquiries. It implies there is a single or static culture. There are multiple cultures which are constantly changing. Culture can change all of the time because there are many moving pieces, many determinants that can impact on a daily basis and even sometimes minute by minute. Culture is not a 'thing' that can be neatly described or managed, it is invisible. However, while it is hard to get a handle on and impossible to measure, people can feel it. And people can feel when it changes – which it can do quite quickly, particularly when there is a significant event, or a shift of leadership.

A good safety culture is one where there is a mindset that human beings are fallible; care can and will go wrong, and when it does there is a need to support those involved and learn about why it happened. Behaviours that sustain a safety culture are positive and supportive including kindness, civility, respect and empathy. Behaviours that hinder a safety culture include incivility and professional rivalry. These behaviours are compounded by poor communication, a chaotic work environment, poorly designed equipment, inadequate staffing levels and high workload.

> We must turn away from the fear culture, the 'us-and-them' culture, the blame and shame culture, the 'super gag to save your skin and to hell with everyone else' culture, the formulaic letter of apology to tick a box compliance culture.
>
> **Scott Morrish**

3.3 Blame, Shame and Fear

How many of us would survive the microscopic scrutiny of our actions? There is almost no human action or decision that cannot be made to look more flawed and less sensible in the misleading light of hindsight.

3.3.1 Blame

When something has gone wrong, there is a strong emotional reaction, and it is very human to blame. We all have the ability to blame others unfairly from time to time in everyday life, including at work. This applies equally to the patient and family as well as the staff. Naturally, the patient and their family want to find out what happened, but they also often want to find out who is responsible and sometimes who is to blame. Staff can also be quick to judge without thinking. Colleagues blame their co-workers for not getting it right; they conclude that it is obviously down to the poor performance of an individual, laziness or carelessness, and this can lead to the individual feeling ostracised and alone.

> We, as humans, are our own worst enemies. We demand fairness from others but have the tendency to unfairly blame others. Blame strangles truth, learning and excellence.

Healthcare has had a long relationship with a culture of blame. The culture attached to 'Safety I' is to tell people what to do and to blame them when they fail. The culture calls for resignations, sackings and even prosecutions from social media, traditional media, the legal system and the general public. We have seen earlier in the book how, in patient safety the complexity, of the system is often ignored and the failure of the human being involved is seen as the single causal focus. As discussed, this is perpetuated by the language of 'human error', or 'team failure'.

Think about when you or someone has a bad day or a bad moment. That individual has potentially worked over 100 twelve-hour shifts in one year and performed tens of thousands of tasks, instructions and interactions. Assuming that they are trained to do the job they are doing and have the appropriate resources and equipment to do that job, one mistake or even a few mistakes would still mean thousands of times when the practitioner got it right.

> But we define ourselves by one bad day, one bad moment or one mistake.

However, it is really important to note that the momentary lapse in performance is not an indicator for their normal level of competence. There may be times when performance varies and there are a number of variables that can trigger this performance drop, but most of these are not down to the individuals themselves. Despite this, the default question when something goes wrong is not what went wrong or how did it go wrong but who was responsible.

The vast majority of frontline practitioners are diligent and thoughtful. When something goes wrong, it is highly likely to be true to say that the same thing has gone right many times before and will go right many times in the future.

If we all think that we have to be perfect, then the opposite of this is that we don't feel that we can fail. So, when we inevitably do fail, we struggle to cope with this and may even wish to hide or cover the failure up. If you are like this, you may also find it hard to trust others to be as perfect as you. People who feel like they have to be strong find it hard to ask for help or admit they can't do something. This can extend to things that they really should ask for help with because by not doing so would be risky or even unsafe. Also, if you feel you have to be strong, you will try to solve problems on your own and lose out on other people's wisdom and ideas.

As humans we have some control over our choices but less control over our mistakes. The Nobel Prize winner Daniel Kahneman has explored the way we make decisions in his book *Thinking, Fast and Slow* (2012). He talks about us having two brains, the system 1 brain for subconscious reasoning and operating automatically or carrying out routine tasks such as riding a bike, driving, walking home, making a cup of tea, and the system 2 brain for conscious reasoning which processes one thing at a time. Our decisions are therefore a combination of subconscious instinctive choices and conscious analytical ones.

> If someone makes a mistake, what good does it do to punish them? Will it make them any safer?

People's actions only make sense when the world they work in, the tasks they are asked to do and the environment they inhabit is deeply understood. Key to this understanding is to learn about what happens naturally, what happens on a day-to-day basis, why it works well most of the time, the work-as-done discussed earlier in Part Two. The more important thing to do is ask why they made a mistake. In order to do that we need to speak to the people involved, really talk to them and listen to their stories. What normally happens, and then what happened at the time of the mistake, all with the intent of learning. Use the tools described in Part Two to help people learn so that others can benefit.

3.3.2 Shame

One of the biggest threats to our self-worth is shame (Brown 2018). Sadly, a lot of people who work in healthcare feel shame, not only when things go wrong but also in not being able to provide the care they would like to provide (Kay 2017). Shame makes us feel we are not worthy of belonging or even love and can lead us to being blamed, put down, ignored or pushed away. The only people who don't experience shame are those who lack the capacity for empathy and human connection (Brown 2018).

People often punish themselves harshly when things go wrong, and this together with the shame associated with the mistake can cause excessive stress, depression, anxiety and ill health. Guilt and self-blame and shame are very common in healthcare. People want to feel pride in where they work, but if they feel shame, then this will seriously affect people's morale as well as their ability to provide care. Shame is intricately connected to safety. The staff member will internalise the shame: 'I must be a really bad person' or 'it was all down to me and I need to do better next time'. People are terrified of being seen as incompetent or stupid. They are deeply ashamed and embarrassed if they don't know what they are doing or things don't go as planned or they do something they should not have. Shame is the intensely painful feeling or experience of believing that we are flawed and therefore unworthy of love, belonging and connection (Brown 2018).

3.3.3 Fear

> Courage and fear are not mutually exclusive. Most of us feel brave and afraid at the exact same time. We feel vulnerable. Sometimes all day long.
>
> **Brené Brown 2018**

Fear is all too real when something has gone wrong. Fear of what other people will think, what our family and friends will think, how we will be judged and what will happen to our reputation and careers. The fear pervades at all levels of the organisation from the board to the frontline. We have to continue working with or alongside these people from one day to the next. Strained relations make for an unpleasant working life. But it is the judgements of those closest to us such as co-workers we are most concerned about (Shorrock 2017).

If the culture is one of fear, then people are likely not to talk to anyone outside their area of what actually goes on, particularly if it is not in accordance with the rules, procedures or policies of where they work. They may fear getting into trouble or finding that others will judge their actions as unacceptable. They are worried about the potential blame that could be associated with that view. These actions, while not known outside of an area, may well be known very well within it. The fear of failing, of making mistakes, not meeting people's expectations and being criticised can be all-consuming. Therefore, disclosing is not only about the personal fear but the fear of disclosing what their co-workers and friends are doing. Actions may be kept hidden in light of the risk or fear of disclosure.

As we discussed earlier, when looking at 'work-as-disclosed' and inspections, all the different approaches to scrutiny and examination currently perpetuate the fear and blame culture associated with improving the safety of healthcare. They take the form of watching people, interviewing them, reviewing various forms of harm data and the operational systems of an organisation. It includes how an organisation is led, how safe it is, how productive and efficient it is and what the experience of those on the receiving end is.

Being involved in an inquiry, a review or complaint or an investigation is highly stressful and in some cases the stress can be too much and can lead to self-harm, burnout and ultimately suicide. There is often a lack of clarity as to why the individual is being investigated by investigators who have limited skills in investigation. The whole thing is adversarial and inquisitorial. There are significant numbers of suspensions and dismissals based on limited or flawed evidence, which perpetuates the blame, shame and fear.

For any amount of scrutiny, the right culture is vital.

Inspection should be used to understand why people behave the way they do, and understanding the person in the organisational context and the wider system is vital. It is equally mistaken to attribute successes to careful planning as it is to attribute failures to individual incompetence or error. The inspection should pay attention to the conditions under which people succeed instead of looking myopically at why things go wrong. To understand the everyday will mean that the inspection understands the multitude of challenging conditions involving demand, pressure, capacity, staffing, competence, equipment, procedures, supplies and time. Only then can the systems, tasks and work processes be redesigned to make it easier for people to work safely.

3.3.4 Impact on Staff

Gupta and his colleagues (2018) surveyed over 65,000 physician mothers on 17 June 2016 of which 5,782 responded. Of those involved in a mistake, 82% reported feelings of guilt, 2.2% reduced their clinical workload, taking leave or leaving the profession (Gupta et al. 2018). In November 2018, there was a story in *The Guardian* newspaper (Anonymous 2018) of a GP sharing what it felt like to be a GP who had made a mistake and was being sued. I found it extremely moving, so rather than describe it here, I think it works better if I simply replicate it below:

> I am the doctor who made a mistake, and you are my patient. You sat in front of me once before and I missed your diagnosis. You sit in front of me again. Anger in your voice, tears in your eyes, as you tell me of the harm I have done to you. Tears are in my eyes too.
>
> Your diagnosis is the sort a GP dreads. Rare. So rare that most GPs will never see a case in their whole career. Insidious, with vague symptoms, hiding in your body until too late. Life-altering or life ending. Cases take an average of six months to be diagnosed. Yours took longer.

There were other doctors, other health professionals who saw you after me. But I was the first to miss
your diagnosis. I saw you less than one week after
your symptoms started. I examined you thoroughly
and found nothing that concerned me. You had me
your anger and your pain. My hands feel empty as
I offer my remorse and my apologies in return. It is
not enough. How could it be? When I find out you
intend to sue, I understand. As you go I feel a piece
of my own life slip away with you. I start to dissolve
at my desk.

In the days after, I am tearful and withdrawn. The
legal letters arrive and start the long process of investigation. It's a strange limbo. I wait to hear if medical
regulator bodies wish to do their own enquires. Will
I be able to continue my career? Will my children see
my face in the papers?

Doctors under investigation by the General
Medical Council have a suicide risk 13 times higher
than that of the general population. I turn these
figures over in my mind, and for the first time I truly
understand them. I know this uncertainty can last
years.

The rhythms of life anchor me – but while I brush
my teeth and read stories, you sit behind me. You are
the first and last thought each day, my only thought
in moments of peace. Family and friends ask what's
wrong but I cannot share. I feel shame, guilt, sadness
and fear. The smell of failure clings to me like smoke.
I no longer know who I am. I read textbooks on
your diagnosis and re-read my own notes from our
first meeting. In honesty, I struggle to see anything I
would change. Somehow that makes it worse.

I know and I knew myself to be a good doctor. I take time and listen. I am knowledgeable and
I share that knowledge so we can decide together

how to care for you. I am the sort of doctor who phones unsolicited after my surgery to check you are ok, who remembers your name and takes a genuine interest in your life.

But a good doctor doesn't make mistakes. A good doctor doesn't get sued. I question my every decision. If I made this mistake, how many more have I made? I cannot trust my judgement. I am not enough. I do not know how to return to work, how to look my patients in the eye, but I have no choice.

I am the UK doctor who should expect to be sued four times in a 40 year career. When I qualified as a doctor that figure was 0.5 times per career. You are my first and I pray that you will also be my last. I am the doctor who made a mistake and I no longer know who I am.

What this GP needed was support, someone he or she could turn to, someone who won't judge them and will seek to understand. They need to know that good doctors do make mistakes and good doctors do get sued. We should also speed up the process of investigation and litigation for people on both sides of the story. This story is the case for countless clinicians. In the aftermath, often distraught clinicians, unsupported by their seniors are made to 'confess to their errors'. They are lonely and frightened, unable to sleep at night. Once you know the outcome, it's hard mitigating the significance of events along the path to a serious incident or even a patient death. It sounds like you are making excuses.

So, rather than define yourself or others by one bad day or one bad moment, think about the many times you have got it right and how many times you are likely to get it right in the future. Make learning about why it happened the most important thing to focus on and not that single moment. When you can do that for yourself, you can also reach out to others and help them. A bit like putting your oxygen mask on first before you put it on your children – help yourself to cope and then help others to do the same. This is an important metaphor for those of you who run around taking care of everything and everyone else except yourself. If you don't take care of yourself, you can experience burnout, stress, fatigue, reduced mental effectiveness, health problems, anxiety, frustration, inability to sleep (and even death). Don't let that happen to you or anyone else.

3.4 Incivility and Bullying

When most people think of bullying, they think of the powerful aggressor, the dominant individual who shouts at people, throws things around and who is verbally and sometimes physically abusive to others. However, this form of bullying is at one end of the spectrum and there is so much more to add to the range of behaviours that could be catergorised as bullying. These behaviours include minor rudeness or incivility to grandstanding, humiliation and intimidation.

3.4.1 Incivility

Incivility is Uncivilised.

Incivility exists in healthcare and is described as 'when people are short or rude'. It can be exhibited in a number of ways, from people being angry, rolling eyes, sneers, interrupting others, shouting and put downs to even simple things like not returning a smile or not saying hello. Examples are varied and include a boss berating an employee, someone walking out of a conversation, people answering calls in the middle of a conversation or meeting or a senior belittling a junior member of the team or people using threats as a way to control behaviours in others. What matters most is how the person on the end of the behaviour feels, i.e., incivility is in the eyes of the recipient (Porath 2016).

Many people have shared their experiences with me of being criticised in front of colleagues, public reprimands and intentional humiliation. It slowly ate away at their self-confidence, their ability to trust those around them, their capacity to think and perform and plunged their morale. They often think it is just them until they hear what I and others are saying in relation to incivility. They think it is something they have done or that they are just too sensitive. They feel ashamed that they cannot cope or deal with it. Most people's tactic is to please the bully or the people being rude, mainly because they do not want to upset them or make it worse. People often have no one to turn to.

The most surprising thing for me in both my own personal experience and hearing that of others is how subtle it is. I remember being in a meeting and I had forgotten to do something and when this was realised the person simply stared at me with a cold long look that went straight to my core. But they didn't just do this for a few seconds, they stared and stared and stared for what felt like minutes. This wasn't the loud shout, the aggressive swearing bully I expected it was a simple and quiet stare.

The people who are 'watching in' look away.

Research has shown that incivility has increased over the last two decades, for example, students are about 30% more narcissistic than the average student 25 years ago. One of the issues Porath (2016) cites is globalisation – a person from one culture may unknowingly behave or speak in a way that offends someone from another culture. Her second factor is that of different attitudes in different generations. The way in which we communicate electronically can also make matters significantly worse. Emails have been used to express anger, to embarrass and to show disrespect. There is a need for email etiquette to rein in the behaviours that have in some respects become out of control. There are many things people can do differently, but in short, be more aware of the tone of the email, be thoughtful and think about the recipient and how they may perceive what is written. Don't use sarcasm or capitals and don't forward emails to make someone look bad.

3.4.2 Impact of Incivility

In order to consider the impact of incivility it is worth taking a look at civility. Civility can be used to shut down anger or to open up conversations. Civility is seen as nice, tame and safe. To use civility to counter rudeness is too simplistic. Civility enables us to be present to start the conversation, but it takes kindness, humility, empathy, trust and respect to take the conversation further. The opposite of incivility is not civility that is behaving in a civil fashion. The opposite is more positive than that, it is respect, dignity, courtesy and kindness.

Incivility can deplete our immune systems and can be as bad for your health as smoking and obesity (Porath 2016). Incivility impacts on people's cognition, their happiness and quality of work and takes its toll on productivity, morale and relationships (Riskin et al. 2015, Porath et al. 2013). People take incivility home and can pass it on, being rude to their friends and family who in turn carry the rudeness on to others. The effects of incivility ripples far beyond the people directly around you – if not careful, it can spiral out of control.

Porath learned in a study of 800 managers who had been on the end of incivility:

48% intentionally decreased their work effort.
47% intentionally decreased the time spent at work.
38% intentionally decreased the quality of their work.
80% lost work time worrying about the incident.
63% lost work time avoiding the offender.
66% said their performance declined.

78% said their commitment to the organisation declined.
12% said that they had left their job because of the incivility.
25% admitted taking their frustration out on their customers.

In an industry like healthcare that is totally reliant on people being able to adjust their performance, make decisions about complex issues and think quickly in order to keep patients safe, incivility has a big negative impact.

The person in authority is three times more likely to be rude. To a patient, that can be everyone. Because we lose our cognitive ability, i.e., we are not smart anymore and have lost the ability to think, the bully will be the smartest person in the room. This perpetuates the feeling that they are 'better' than those they are surrounded by. Instead choose to behave in ways that help people feel less intimidated.

In one study, 24 medical teams from four neonatal intensive care units in Israel were assigned to care for a premature infant using simulation training. Half of the teams received messages from a neutral expert who did not comment on the quality of their work. The other half received insulting messages about their performance. The teams exposed to the rudeness displayed lower capabilities in all diagnostic and procedural performance metrics, 'markedly diminishing the infant's chances of survival' (Porath 2016). The teams who were exposed to rudeness didn't share information as readily and they also stopped seeking help from their teammates.

3.4.3 Bullying

One in five NHS doctors and a quarter of other NHS staff are said to have been victims of bullying or harassment. Similar to as with incivility, they describe a loss of confidence, taking time off work, a struggle to function, trouble sleeping, feeling physically sick and emotionally broken. The more the rudeness and bullying happens the less people want to be at work. People actively search for a new role and become quite desperate to move on. They also start to become the person that the 'bully' perceived, their performance deteriorates, and they forget or miss deadlines and are not particularly good at their job. This fuels the bully who thinks they were right all along. At a certain point they start not to care and, in some instances, deliberately shut down. This can lead to even worse feelings of shame and despair and as mentioned earlier, in rare cases to them taking their own life.

> People shut down if they lack a sense of psychological safety, and they are less likely to seek or accept feedback or to discuss errors or speak up about potential or actual problems – the very opposite of what we want in a culture of safety.

Bullying affects different groups, especially those of diverse cultures, ethnicities or religion; these minorities are often the ones who are treated more harshly. Many people from different cultures tend to be deferential to authority, with doctors and nurses from ethnic minorities being excessively deferential to hierarchy and institutions. When growing up, they are repeatedly told by their elders, that they should not rock the boat and that they should be grateful that they are living in Britain, grateful and honoured that they are physicians. This is why doctors from such cultures can so easily find themselves unstuck when errors happen (Kline 2018).

This division between different professions also perpetuates a lack of trust and erodes relationships between people and, as a result, people are rude to each other. Another form of bullying is the behaviours used to get things done; they can be both harsh – being tough with people – and 'charming' – making people feel they have to do something because it is the right thing to do or will help the person asking. When this is a superior, someone in power, then the inferior has to say yes. Bullying with a smile.

3.4.4 What Can We Do?

There is a clear business case for addressing incivility and its opposite behaviour, kindness. Incivility costs money in terms of workplace stress, loss of workdays, workplace accidents due to stress and reduced effort. Even if people are subjected to low-intensity incivility, research has found that they are not able to concentrate well. Incivility decreases your cognitive resources and your performance. Rudeness affects your mind in ways you might not even be aware of, disrupting your ability to pay attention. If you wanted to perform your best, you can't because you are bothered and preoccupied by the rudeness.

If people are being rude, we need to get curious and try to figure out why without judging. If the behaviour continues, then we need to dig deeper. It is easy to believe that the person is just being difficult, but actually we have not gone deep enough if we just come to that conclusion. Porath asserts that most incivility arises not from malice but from ignorance and that people don't actually want to hurt others and in many instances may not be aware that their actions are hurtful. When we explore we need to really listen. People are often aggrieved that their co-workers that they deem 'incompetent' or 'lazy' or 'don't care' are not being tackled. This means that they are resorting to judgements which in turn can lead to incivility, rudeness and bullying. Instead, there is a need for a conversation that gets beyond the surface of what is going on.

Gerald Hickson (2012) describes a variety of things that can be done and the different levels of response to different behaviours. For example, if there is a single concern, then that could be responded to with an informal conversation, but if there is an apparent pattern or the pattern persists, then there are a variety of interventions that are required. He, like others, is clear that this should be tackled in a non-judgemental way, with a seeking to understand and help the people exhibiting poor behaviour to understand the impact they make but also to see where they can be supported and helped to deal with it. Most people are rude for reasons, and they are rude very rarely. The number of people who are persistently rude is much less.

Dealing with incivility and bullying at work should be a priority for leaders everywhere. For behaviours such as incivility, Brené Brown (2018) says this requires setting some boundaries. For example, telling people it is ok to be angry, but shouting is not ok or being frustrated is ok but interrupting and rolling your eyes is not ok. High-performing teams promote a culture of honesty, authenticity and safe conflict. The behaviours that can counter incivility are often relatively small: smiling more and saying hello in the hallway, saying thank you, recognising what people do, listening with intent. To shift from incivility to a kinder culture, everyone needs to counter the rudeness by role modelling the right behaviour, rewarding good behaviour and dealing with bad behaviour (Porath and Pearson 2013)

> Incivility is the enemy of building a safety culture, 'Safety II' and a restorative just culture.

3.5 Just Culture

> People are not a problem to control, but a solution to harness.
>
> **Dekker 2012**

As Professor James Reason said, whenever he went some-where new, he sought to understand the people and the environment with a view to learn and not to be judgemental. Being non-judgemental is crucial for investigators and for a restorative just culture. Proportionality is crucial for a just culture. If people are judged unfairly and sanctioned in a way that is clearly disproportionate it creates fear and can lead to people not speaking up. It can also lead to poor rela-tionships and a loss of trust between different people in the organisation.

> Seek not to judge, but at least to understand.

Our healthcare system is designed in a way to try to man-age the people who I referred to earlier who are considered reckless or worse, criminal. The people who intend to harm patients. However, this is a tiny minority. Over the period that the NHS has been in existence (70 years) there have been probably around 20 or 30 people who fit the 'intentional harm' or 'criminal category'. This is within a service of over a mil-lion staff. While of course we need to have systems that can detect these people, we also need to help and support the vast majority of the million people who do not intend to harm. That is why we need a consistent approach to the implemen-tation of a just culture and the proportionate response to the way in which people behave and act which leads on to the restorative just culture.

3.5.1 *Just Culture*

A just culture is the balance of fairness, justice and account-ability. Just culture 'is a culture in which front-line operators and others are not punished for actions, omissions or deci-sions taken by them which are commensurate with their experience and training, but where gross negligence, wilful violations and destructive acts are not tolerated' (Eurocontrol 2018). It assumes that human beings are fallible, make mistakes whether in their personal or professional lives and the vast majority always try to do the best they can. A just culture provides a framework which shifts the focus from blaming individuals to understanding why things went wrong and is based on the principle that professionals should not be punished for unintentional acts. However, a just culture should not be just about when things have gone wrong, or about safety, it is needed all of the time. It is intricately linked to equity, equality, diversity, inclusivity and justice.

> If the view is that safety is about 'when things go wrong' and failure i.e. 'safety I', then there is a need to protect the people involved from being unjustly blamed. In that respect a just culture is the consequence of a 'safety I' view of the world.
>
> **Hollnagel 2016**

In a 'Safety II' view of the world, a just culture is about recognising that work is based on adjustments and adaptation and that people should be treated fairly as a result. Hollnagel (2016) believes it should be termed a 'fair culture'. A fair culture attempts to understand the prescribed world and the reality and the gap in between. It recognises that people have to be flexible and adjust what they do. A fair culture is one where there is no bias from hindsight or outcome. It is not fair to blame people for decisions that sometimes work and sometimes don't. However, in his view, because we live in a predominantly 'Safety I' world there is still a need for a just culture.

David Marx (2016), a just culture expert, believes that a just culture is the balance between accountability and learning and the proportionate response to when things go wrong. It is about supporting practitioners who make mistakes but sanction someone who consciously takes an irresponsible risk. Marx distinguishes three behavioural concepts: human error, risky behaviour and reckless conduct. In simple terms he views the response to the three different components of the just culture as:

■ Human error: the inadvertent actions or decisions which lead to unintended outcomes (mistakes, slips, lapses):
  – Marx views 'human error' as actions or decisions made by people going about their day-to-day tasks; they occur when they are bored and when they are busy, when they are pressured and when they are not. We are now aware of how stress, distractions, being unfocused, being too busy and not being busy enough can all lead to an increased propensity to error. In fact, those that have erred are more likely to do it again because of the stress caused by the first error.
■ Risky behaviour: where people make particular choices that are on a spectrum of risk from low to high risk:
  – Risky behaviour is defined as choices and decisions we make when we are under pressure. Most treatments come with a set of risks: risk of complications or side effects, for example. In discussions with patients, decisions are made as to whether the risk is justified or acceptable. Hollnagel would suggest that this is simply getting things done. Marx believes that a risky choice is purposeful rather than forgetful. However, some people are heightened to the potential risks around them and others don't really notice them. We have different attitudes to, and different interpretations of, risk.
  – How we make decisions and how we manage our risky behaviours are affected by whether the issues or tasks are new or something that has been done time

and time before, it is affected by whether we are tired, hungry, bored, stressed, distracted or overwhelmed. For example, the more people are exposed to risky situations, the more they get used to being in the risky situations, the more complacent they may be in making the choices they make.

- Some risky behaviour or policy 'violations' will be the right thing to do. Examples of risky behaviour in healthcare may be omitting a double check for a medication because the nurse knows who his or her patient is. Or the surgeon who does not believe in the 'time out' in surgery because he or she has never operated on the wrong patient or the wrong body part. Or the nurse who does not check the patient's identification because he or she is too busy and has done the same thing loads of times before without it going wrong.

■ Reckless behaviour: where people cross a line from making a risky choice to making a reckless choice where they know that their actions will be unsafe – the conscious disregard of a substantial and unjustifiable risk:
- Reckless behaviour is often referred to as gross negligence and involves a higher degree of culpability than negligence. It is described as a conscious disregard by a healthcare practitioner for the risk to the patients, or themselves or their colleagues. Recklessness or reckless behaviour could result from a continuation or extension of risky behaviour.
- Examples include drink driving, driving at excessive speed, performing surgery while intoxicated, conducting a clinical treatment that you have no idea how to perform and have not been trained in, and using new drugs or equipment without seeking help. Consider you are driving and you see a car ahead both speeding and weaving in and out of lanes. The car is violating traffic rules and taking a risk which could cause an

accident. It is highly likely that the driver knows the risk they are taking.

– Some people view the 'not reporting an error' or 'trying to cover up errors or incidents' as reckless behaviour.

– The response to reckless behaviour is for the individual to take responsibility for their actions and to be called to account. This is the extreme end of a just culture spectrum and is the only time when the individual requires discipline, sanction and punishment. If there is a view that the clinician was reckless, then they should be reported to the professional regulator, and or the judicial/criminal authorities – who will deal with him or her. This is why the just culture is not a blame free culture.

3.5.2 Clinical Negligence

Clinical negligence, another distinction we like to make on people's performance, is defined as a breach of the duty of care owed to a patient that has led to harm. It is a legal term for conduct that falls below the standard required for patients. There is a test of 'reasonableness' which is used to judge whether the person's performance was reasonable. The legal system has to prove that there was a duty of care and that harm was caused by the negligent action of others. Dekker rightly asks:

What is normal standard?
How far is below?
What is reasonable?
Was harm indeed caused by negligent action?

However, this gets confused with 'reckless behaviour'. For example, as David Marx says, if you participate in sports, which is a high-risk system, and you make a mistake and break the ankle of your fellow football player, the person who gets harmed has to deal with it. It's the cost of doing business to participate in the high-risk endeavour of sport. But if the player is deemed reckless, the sport says that you have a cause of action against that person, that is, you should pay for my broken ankle because you were reckless.

Healthcare has an analogy to sport, in the sense that it is filled with imperfect human beings and is a very high-risk industry. Clinicians are going to make mistakes; they are fallible. But it hasn't changed the legal system, which says if you get harmed by the medical system, you should sue. Marx believes that the underlying logic is flawed. His view is that we have to believe that healthcare institutions are going to produce bad outcomes. They're going to be fallible, and we need a compensation system that doesn't rely on having to sue the hospital or doctor. For example, in New Zealand, there is the Accident Compensation Scheme for when there is a case of clinical negligence.

3.5.3 *Accountability and Responsibility*

These terms can often be used to mean the same thing and are used interchangeably in a lot of safety work, in the main 'you are accountable to' and 'responsible for' (Dekker 2010). In safety, people are accountable to patients and their families, those who manage and lead and those who scrutinise and regulate. Accountable to these people to say sorry, to inform, to explain and to follow up. Responsibility is in the form of learning – people are responsible for learning from what happened. People can also be responsible for being accountable.

A just culture is the balance of safety, accountability and responsibility. Accountability is not just being 'accountable to', it is to ensure that there is an account of what happened. A just culture means getting an account of what went on to satisfy the demands for accountability and one that will contribute to learning and improvement.

Responsibility can get confused with blame, i.e., someone is responsible for what happened. In this respect, when it comes to responsibility it is important to ask 'what' is responsible, not 'who' is responsible.

3.5.4 Who Gets to Draw the Line?

Dekker is well known for asking 'who gets to draw the line'. As he says, the just culture concept has often tried to draw the line between acceptable and unacceptable behaviour. For example, wilful acts, intentional acts and recklessness are not acceptable. Error, mistakes, and unintentional acts are acceptable. But who gets to draw the line between error, risky behaviour and reckless behaviour? Can we clearly distinguish between the three behaviours? What about the subjective nature of this, the different biases that we have as human beings and the way in which one person's view of a behaviour may be different from another? Categorising other people's behaviours appears simple but in fact is difficult. Try answering some of these questions:

What would you define as error versus risky versus reckless behaviour?
When does an error become risky behaviour?
Who do you think has the authority to draw the line?
Who would you like to be judged by?

Judging someone as erroneous or risky or reckless is 'our' judgement of what other people do, not a description of their behaviour. Too often the review of in incident is used as a way of highlighting an individual's performance or capability in general rather than in relation to the incident. Incident investigations are not appraisals or performance reviews.

3.5.5 *Restorative Just Culture*

Dekker's view is that we need more than a 'just culture'; we need a 'restorative just culture'.

Dekker believes the focus should be on who was hurt and what is needed to restore the damage, trust and relationships. He says if we really want a just culture, then we have to empathise with others and understand why what they did made sense to them at the time, try to understand the situation they were in and their world from their view. The aim is to shift from a retributive just culture, which is a 'blunt HR or managerial instrument to get rid of people'. A retributive culture asks which rule was broken, how bad is it and who is to blame and holds a person accountable when things go wrong and asks who was to blame, why did they behave in that way and why did they make such a risky decision? Society, the public, patients and their families may want some sort of retribution. Retributive justice focuses on the errors or violation and seeks a way to punish the individual or individuals involved. Instead we should focus on healing described as a restorative culture. It takes a strong and confident person to suggest that in fact what is needed is a more healing approach. This is where multiple stories and points of view are explored including that of the patient and their families. An assumption is made that no one intended to harm anyone, no one intended to mess things up or make a mistake. The approach is constructive and consists of developing strong relationships, ongoing dialogue and openness between all parties.

Instead, what we should do is respond to signs of failure with compassion and a desire to learn. Dekker talks about building a restorative just culture with the aim of repairing trust and relationships damaged after an incident. He has devised a restorative just culture checklist (Dekker 2019) which asks three powerful questions:

Who was hurt?
What do they need?
Whose obligation is it to meet the need?

3.5.6 Who Was Hurt?

Asking 'who was hurt' asks us to think deeply about who could be affected following the incident. Of course, it is the patient and their loved ones, but even this doesn't do justice to the number of people affected in relation to the patient. The ripple effect can mean that 'who was hurt' can include the patient's friends, their extended family, their neighbours and the local community. When something goes wrong, people naturally want to talk about it and share their experience. This in turn spreads across people and communities and can ultimately affect the way in which people view and have confidence in their local healthcare providers.

If we take the notion that the ripple effect also impacts on staff, then 'who was hurt' can include the immediate staff members, their co-workers, their friends and family, their managers, leaders, mentors, teachers and then others in the vicinity the support workers, the cleaners, porters and receptionists. If we take it even further, in my experience for some incidents, 'who was hurt' can include the entire organisation or an entire profession. The impact and memory of an incident can be felt for many years.

3.5.7 What Do They Need?

'What do they need' asks us to think about every individual and to be mindful that they all may want something different. The only way this will be known is to sit down and ask them. This starts the conversation right at the beginning in a way that is about restoring confidence and ensuring that individual needs are understood and met. One person may want lots of information immediately; others may want to be left alone for a while. Some staff may want to be sent home; others may want to stay. Think about what the person needs for themselves, not what you think they need.

3.5.8 Whose Obligation Is It to Meet the Need?

'Whose obligation is it to meet the need' reminds us that it is incredibly important to assign people to both the family and the staff for as long as it takes. Ensure that they have someone to talk to, go to and find out information from. We should never leave people wondering what is happening. This will help in some part to ensure that the situation does not become adversarial and inquisitorial.

A restorative just culture does not mean a lack of accountability or responsibility, and it doesn't mean that people need to be blamed. Blame implies a sanction: suspension, disciplinary action, removal or even dismissal. This does little to instil a sense of justice for anyone, in fact, it simply instils a sense of anxiety and fear which leads to silence. Accountability is achieved by people accounting for themselves, their actions and providing as much detail as possible for everyone. Accountability is achieved by being open and fair to all. Responsibility is achieved when changes are made, and systems are made safer as a result. One key aspect is to say sorry. By apologising, you start on the road to a restorative just culture. Some people find this easier than others. There is little more restorative in a relationship than an honest and unreserved apology.

3.5.9 Mersey Care Partnership

The goals of restorative justice are accepting appropriate responsibility for what happened, to deal with feelings of grief, resentment, humiliation, guilt and shame, to repair trust and relationships, to help people get back to work and to address the causes of harm. Some of the aims of the restorative just culture movement are to freeze suspensions of staff, throw out the disciplinary policy in relation to error and identify the downward pressures that create fear. The incentives to have a restorative just culture are very simple. It increases staff morale and job satisfaction and people will as a result be more productive. Without it you will not know what is going on and your staff will not perform as well as they could . There is both justice and learning for the patients and the people that care for them.

An evolving example of creating a restorative just culture can be seen at Mersey Care Partnership Trust in the UK. Their story so far is shared in a 20-minute film which you can find via www.sidneydekker.com/justculture. It is a deeply moving film which charts the work of HR Director Amanda Oates and her colleagues in their goal of shifting the culture of blame to one of learning. The CEO of the organisation, Joe Rafferty, talks about how they felt they had to do something, that suspending staff drives learning underground and in order to bring learning to the surface the organisation needed a just culture. However, he and Amanda stress that they are at the start of learning how to do this and it has to fit for each organisation – you cannot buy it off the shelf. When something goes wrong at Mersey Care they aim to provide true support for colleagues, have a rapid debrief that enables some quick learning before going any further. They also work on an early resolution for patients and ensure that they offer a genuine and heartfelt apology. They have given permission for junior colleagues to challenge senior colleagues and to 'stop the process' if they can. As a result of this work, their suspension rates are reduced by nearly 90%, and they have reduced the cost of dealing with suspensions and reduced absenteeism, with the associated financial savings.

> If you want to change behavior, don't target behavior. Target the conditions under which it takes place. Those conditions are not likely the worker's responsibility.
>
> **Dekker 2017a**

3.6 Part Three Summary

Part Three has shared my reflections and that of others in relation to culture, blame, shame, fear and incivility. The conclusion is that we have to take the blame out of failure. There is almost no human action or decision that cannot be made to look more flawed and less sensible in the misleading light of hindsight, yet we define people by their one bad day or one bad moment. Yet, the vast majority of frontline practitioners are diligent and thoughtful. When something goes wrong, it is highly likely to be true to say that the same thing has gone right many times before and will go right many times in the future.

We must urgently address the incivility and bullying within healthcare. I think this is one of the most important priorities for leaders in all areas of healthcare. Over the last two years, I have had the chance to speak to thousands of healthcare staff from all professions and all care settings. The abiding feeling I have had from these interactions is the struggle people are having with incivility and bullying. Staff are feeling isolated and lonely and experience incivility frequently. For some it has migrated to bullying and harassment. This, together with the blame culture across healthcare, is impacting on staff morale, staff satisfaction and relationships. It is impacting on people's ability to work safely. These behaviours can lead to a decrease in work effort, time spent at work, quality of work and performance. They increase stress, worry and anxiety and may result in people leaving their jobs and profession.

In an industry like healthcare that is totally reliant on people being able to adjust their performance, make decisions about complex issues and think quickly in order to keep patients safe, incivility and bullying have a big negative impact. However, there is hope. There are a variety of ways in which we can work differently to tackle the problem of incivility and bullying. The restorative just culture also provides a way in which we can respond proportionately to when things do not go as planned. It provides the beautiful balance of fairness with support and with accountability. In order to support the restorative just culture all you need to do is ask and find the answers for the following three powerful questions:

Who was hurt?
What do they need?
Whose obligation is it to meet the need?

3.7 Part Three Actions

A few actions to urgently tackle the culture of blame are:

- Understand the spectrum of behaviours from incivility to bullying and develop a strategy for your organisation on how you will address these.
- Those responsible for 'judging others' within your organisation (the HR staff, the line managers, the investigators) must be trained in the different concepts and methods for building a restorative just culture.
- Create a policy which sets out clearly what actions will be taken for staff when things go wrong , which describes clearly what your organisation will do to bring to life the three questions:
  - Asking who was hurt
  - Asking what they need
  - Being clear about whose obligation it is to meet those needs

- Find someone you trust, someone you know will not judge you no matter what and ask them to be there for you when things will inevitably go wrong.
- Always seek support when things have gone wrong – do not suffer in silence.
- For anyone you work for, work with or lead – ask them what they need when something goes wrong.
- Keep everyone informed during any investigation (incident or complaint – patient and staff member) even if you do not know anything – do everything you can to prevent the situation becoming both adversarial for patients and inquisitorial for staff.
- Consider rewriting your disciplinary policy to remove disciplinary actions related to error.
- Notice the people around you, are they withdrawing, hiding or silencing themselves – seek them out and ask them if they are ok. If someone has the courage to share their experience with you, listen, reach out and connect for as long as they need.
- If it is happening to you, it is highly likely to be happening to others – you are not alone – reach out to people you trust to share – battling in silence will not help.
- One selfish mindset will infect a collective culture. It is kind to address those that are not being part of the team or are causing friction and tension within the team. It is kind to try to find out why before judging.
- When talking to people who are exhibiting poor behaviours – avoid being judgemental, acknowledge there are two sides to any story, stick to facts, steer away from the emotions and name the behaviour and describe how those behaviours are affecting others – show empathy and end with encouragement.
- Have a conversation that is respectful, confidential, non-directive, non-defensive, and collegial and in a private space – anticipate the 'push back' e.g.,

- Deflection – it's not me …
- Dismissal – I don't believe …
- Distraction – we really should be focusing on …
- Respond respectfully – it is not about control or power or being defensive back – it is about the goal of the conversation a) an observation was made b) I am sharing that with you.

■ Describe a single behaviour and observation to really help the recipient think about that behaviour rather than a blanket, sweeping assessment of their behaviour – the more specific you can be, the more they can learn from it.

■ Ask for feedback on your behaviours from people you trust – it may be that you are not aware that you may also be behaving rudely and in that respect think about how you talk to others but also how you communication electronically – think about how your emails may be misinterpreted – if in doubt don't send it.

■ If you feel yourself being rude or frustrated or stressed – you do not have to be brutal, or aggressive or rude to get things done – you don't have to hide your rudeness by simply saying 'I tell it how it is' – at all times talk to people how you would want to be talked to –. be empathetic of others feelings

■ Take care of yourself, your health and wellbeing and the triggers that might lead to you being rude.

■ Give any kind of feedback with kindness and respect, treat people in the same way that you would want to be treated; smile more and listen with intent.
  - Give feedback by sitting alongside or walking alongside someone rather than facing each other which can make it adversarial.
  - Giving feedback is as much about listening and asking questions than talking at someone.

- Acknowledge what people do well instead of just picking apart their mistakes.
- Recognise people's strengths.
- Use the feedback to help someone grow.
- Give productive and respectful feedback.
- Genuinely thank someone for their efforts.

Care for the People that Care

We each have a part to play in choosing the values and behaviour that guide our relationships, and we each have the power to SUPPORT THE PEOPLE WE WORK WITH

4.1 Part Four Introduction

Part Four is an essential part of patient safety and makes absolute sense when it is built on and understood in relation to the previous sections. Everything I have spoken about so far helps towards caring for the people that care. Having a 'Safety II' approach 'takes the blame out of failure' and helps people learn in a much more positive way. The latest models aim to understand people's real work experiences and what it feels like to work where they do, to truly understand what they do. Narrowing the gap between work-as-done and work-as-imagined goes further to understand, accept and work with variation rather than dismiss it or try to eliminate it. 'Safety II' helps the people who work in healthcare because it gets beneath the surface and superficiality that 'Safety I' is in order to explain error and complexity. It helps lift them from the shame and blame associated with their errors and actions. The three models of safety help us understand the different needs of the different staff within the ultra-safe, ultra-reliable and ultra-adaptive settings.

We have also explored how a much more positive and proactive way to measure and monitor safety can reduce the burden on frontline staff and, in turn, help leaders understand the safety in their organisations so much more. We have studied the culture and language needed in order to help people work safely and be the very best they can be.

Why care for the people that care?

Part of building resilient systems and teams is to look after the health and wellbeing of staff and to care about them. This is the ultimate means to helping people work safely. In fact, it should be the central driver to any patient safety strategy. The people who work in organisational development and human resources on workforce issues should be connected up with the people who work in safety. Not only will this help people work safely, but it will also tackle the underlying cultures that are hindering safety such as incivility and bullying. It will also build the healing and restorative cultures that have been shown to enhance safety.

It feels simple to me.

How can staff work safely if they have not eaten anything substantial for 12 hours, how can they function if they fail to drink properly, how can they make safe decisions when they are so tired they have forgotten what day of the week it is, how can we help people work safely who have not had a good night's sleep for weeks, how can they be helped to safely carry out complex tasks when their minds are so tired, confused and distracted? How can they speak up or ask for help if they are intimidated and frightened? By supporting our workforce, they can become a force for work.

Caring is not simply about their health and wellbeing. Caring is about supportive leadership, making workplaces positive, bringing joy to people's work and increasing their morale. It is about being kind and showing empathy, appreciation and gratitude. These things have been shown to increase staff engagement and morale and in turn their productivity and quality of work.

And finally, in Part Three, we have tried to explore the aspects that bring toxicity to the workplace culture and erode safety. I have called for an urgency in addressing the very real issues of incivility and blame and their impact on staff wellbeing. Part Four comes with its own sense of urgency: to create the opposite kind of workplace, one that is filled with joy, kindness, empathy, appreciation and gratitude.

> Safer care is only possible if we care for those who care for patients.

4.2 Positivity and Joy

There is a growing recognition of the importance of kindness, positive relationships and focusing on staff health and wellbeing for helping people work safely.

In Part One, I explored the impact of the negative way in which people see our society and in the way in which people view healthcare and safety. As I have mentioned earlier, when we get negative feedback, we hold on to it, we ruminate over it, we put it on a pedestal. Before we can even accept positive feedback, we need to learn to deal with the negative. It isn't a question of shielding ourselves from it, but we can stop it from invading our every thought. To not define ourselves by that one bad day or that one negative comment or the person who put us down. The narrative we use changes how we feel and what we do. We need to bring to the surface the positive narratives which are often ignored.

4.2.1 Positive Emotions

In order for a more positive approach to safety to flourish, it is worth studying the psychology of positive emotions, drawing from =Fredrickson's work *Broaden and Build* (Fredrickson 1998, 2000, 2001, 2004, 2013 and Cawsey et al. 2018). To draw explicit attention to the positive rather than simply look for the negative or even at the absence of the negative, we may in turn help people feel happiness and joy and also develop new insights and ideas. The *Broaden and Build* theory of positive emotions suggests that positive emotions, i.e., enjoyment, happiness, wellbeing and joy, all broaden one's awareness of our surroundings and what we do and in turn encourage creativity, new insights, thoughts and actions. Over time, this broadened behavioural range builds personal skills and resources. This is in contrast to negative emotions, which prompt narrow, immediate survival 'fight or flight' behaviours (Fredrickson 1998, 2000, 2001, 2004, 2013).

Fredrickson has conducted randomised controlled lab studies in which participants are randomly assigned to watch films that induce positive emotions, such as amusement and contentment, or negative emotions, such as fear and sadness, or no emotions. Compared to people in the other conditions, participants who experienced positive emotions showed heightened levels of creativity, inventiveness and 'big picture' perceptual focus. Studies have shown that positive emotions play a role in the development of long-term psychological resilience and flourishing (Fredrickson 2013).

> Positive and authentic feedback instils pride in the workforce, and there are benefits to both the person giving and receiving of saying a simple thank you.
>
> **Frederickson 2013**

4.2.2 Positive Stories

Munro, Chief Executive of Care Opinion in the UK, believes that positive stories really matter (2018). He runs an opinion website about healthcare in the UK and says that people feel that his site is not sharing enough negative stories and that the positive stories cannot contribute to the task of improving care.

> It's almost as if people believe that we only learn and improve when things go badly and can make no progress when things go well.
>
> **Munro 2018**

He cites some great reasons why you would want to learn from the positive stories:

- People like sharing their experiences no matter whether they are positive or negative.
- Listen and learn what it is that matters and why.
- The stories can have a powerful impact on lifting staff morale.
- Online feedback is not just data; it is often an intervention, an act of encouragement, support and solidarity with public service staff.
- Positive stories can be shared widely and can become a simple and effective way to share good practice.
- Positive stories can be a way staff can learn from patients.
- Positive feedback can change the team culture and can provide important insights that contribute to healthcare improvement.

4.2.3 Joy

Positive emotions, positive deviance and positive stories lead naturally on to considering 'joy'. I would define joy as a feeling of great pleasure and happiness and to 'enjoy' is to 'take delight and pleasure in'. Feeling joyful for me is 'feeling, expressing, or causing great pleasure and happiness'. So you can see, joy is closely linked to pleasure and happiness. Psychologists have found that happy people live secure in the knowledge that the activities that bring them enjoyment in the present will also lead to a fulfilling future. This in itself starts to build a more positive workplace. If you ask people what makes them happy they start to really light up and tell you about how much they enjoy what they do, how they like the people they work with and in healthcare a big one is how proud they are to work in an institution or organisation that makes a difference to people's lives.

If you ask them what that feels like or can they give examples, these are often small moments in the day. The smile from someone in the corridor, the meaningful thank you for something you did, the ability to laugh and have fun and learning something new. A lot of people talk about the other people, the relationships. How these relationships can be enhanced by the way we talk to each other in a positive way, the way we smile and show kindness. These include simple acts of asking people how they are, making them a cup of tea or coffee or opening the door for someone who is struggling with case notes and clearly in a hurry. There is something in all of this as well for me, which is about role modelling, the type of leadership needed to create a positive workplace which is tied in with empathy, emotional intelligence and humility. No one should be above making a drink for someone else when they need it.

So why do people think joy and particularly 'joy in work' is important? Survey after survey shows that the morale of staff who work in healthcare is low. One way to improve morale is to foster bringing joy to people's lives, helping them develop friendships, having fun and creating a positive environment. It costs very little to implement.

> The gifts of hope, confidence, and safety that health care should offer patients and families can only come from a workforce that feels hopeful, confident, and safe. Joy in work is an essential resource for the enterprise of healing.
>
> **Berwick in 'Joy in Work' (Perlo et al. 2017)**

The Institute for Healthcare Improvement developed a white paper – the 'IHI Framework for Improving Joy in

Work'. Within this there is a summary that I will lift in totality because it provides a really great summary for me:

> With increasing demands on time, resources, and energy, in addition to poorly designed systems of daily work, it's not surprising health care professionals are experiencing burnout at increasingly higher rates, with staff turnover rates also on the rise. Yet, joy in work is more than just the absence of burnout or an issue of individual wellness; it is a system property. It is generated (or not) by the system and occurs (or not) organization-wide. Joy in work – or lack thereof – not only impacts individual staff engagement and satisfaction, but also patient experience, quality of care, patient safety, and organizational performance.

The 'IHI Framework' (Perlo et al 2017) helps leaders create joy in work by paying attention to the way they behave and how they want others to behave and to consider the critical components that follow:

■ Physical and psychological safety – including equity and a just culture that is safe and respectful.
■ Meaning and purpose – so that daily work is connected to the individual's values, goals and constancy of purpose.
■ Autonomy and control – so that the environment supports choice and flexibility in daily lives and work.
■ Recognition and reward – which shows that people understand daily work, recognising what people are doing and celebrating outcomes.
■ Participative management – co-production, being listened to and provided a space to talk and involvement before change – clear communication and consensus building as part of decision making.
■ Camaraderie and teamwork – social cohesion, productive teams, shared understanding and trusting relationships.

- Daily improvement – proactive learning from failure and success.
- Wellness and resilience – health and wellness, cultivating resilience and stress management, role modelling, values, system appreciation for whole person and family, understanding and appreciation of work life balance, mental health support.
- Real time measurement – regular feedback.

If we link back, therefore, to the definition of joy what else can we find to help us understand the impact of joy on the workplace?

Joy is the most vulnerable emotion we feel. When we feel joy it is a place of incredible vulnerability, its beauty and fragility and deep gratitude and impermanence all wrapped up in one experience.

Brown 2018

Another aspect of joy is our environment, which makes a massive difference to how we feel – the physical characteristics of our spaces shape our emotions. Studies have shown that people who work in colourful environments feel safer and are more alert, confident and friendlier. In fact, orange stimulates mental activity, green reflects growth, yellow is associated with joy, happiness, intellect and energy and red with energy and power. However, hospitals and healthcare buildings in the main don't naturally bring us joy. Think of children's hospitals or clinics, they are full of joy: colour, toys to play with, murals on the walls, interactive games and so on. But this is not the same for all of our other patients who are treated in concrete, white or grey buildings with long and impersonal corridors and doors. This is not great for the patients but the staff who work there are exposed to this same 'dullness' and energy sapping environment every day.

Literally building on this concept is the need to design spaces so that people can engage with others and not just with their own 'group' but across other professions; the vast multidisciplinary people that work in healthcare. We need to help people develop close working friendships not just 'people you work with'. Research shows that people are happier in their jobs when they get on with their co-workers. Friends at work form strong social networks and help each other in the good times and in the bad, they provide advice and support for different situations. Close working friendships increase employee satisfaction by 50%, and people with a close friend at work are seven times more likely to engage fully with their work (Riordan 2013). If we want people to develop working friendships and to work safely, we have to create a more positive culture and workplace.

At the Whittington Hospital in London in the UK, they have introduced time in the day to focus on fun in their emergency department. These included improvisation, painting, origami and sharing information about each other, all to help people focus, multitask and connect with each other. The sessions are very popular, and over time every member of staff has had the opportunity to spend one day immersed in creativity and fun, learning skills that would help them become more resilient as individuals in the high-pressure environment of their work. More than 80% of the staff scored themselves 8/10 on a wellbeing scale, sickness among nursing staff dropped by 30% and staff turnover had more than halved over the year. Giving staff just a small amount of time and space to be together and have fun was found to be uplifting and morale boosting. Connections need to happen somewhere – think about where that could be in your organisation. People felt that they were able to connect to each other in a different and more positive way. Staff even felt appreciated for their personality and their talent and not just their clinical skills.

Consideration should also be given to designing the way in which people move around healthcare organisations, it isn't always simply getting from 'a to b'. To help you think differently about designing your workplace that actually enhances joy and happiness, we can learn from Daniele Quercia (2015). Quercia challenges us to confront some of our daily habits.

> If you think that adventure is dangerous, try routine. It's deadly.
>
> **Quercia (2015)**

So many of us take the same route to work every day, possibly using maps on our smartphones, without really stopping to think whether a better route exists, a more beautiful route, even a happier route. But after taking a detour on his bicycle one day, Quercia (2015) found a beautiful, quiet route that only took him a minute or two longer than his usual, busy, grey route. Quercia said that after this experience he became fascinated with the ways in which people can enjoy a city and started to use computer science tools to replicate social science. The result of that research has been the creation of new maps, maps where you don't only find the shortest path … but also the most enjoyable path. If you visit his website '*Happy Maps*' you can see the way in which his team have created the shortest, happiest, most beautiful or quietest ways to get from the same 'a to b'. It just might make you think differently the next time you go for a walk or affect the way in which you walk around your organisation.

And finally, the team at Kaleidoscope have published a paper 'Beyond Burnout' (Kaleidoscope 2018) which builds on and explores how people can implement the IHI Joy in Work Framework and provides five ways to bring joy right away:

- Eat together – make dedicated time for colleagues, even just five minutes to share a cup of tea or your lunch.
- Say thank you – create a culture of positivity at the workplace by normalising 'thank you' and you will start to hear them back.
- Learn new things – learn things about your work, your patients and each other, discovering something new is invigorating and joyful.
- Support flexibility – do your best not to micromanage your colleagues, let their creativity and joy flourish but be available for advice and direction if needed.

4.2.4 Positivity, Joy and Safety

How does positivity and joy impact on safety? There is a consistent trend from studies examining culture and patient outcomes about how positive cultures are related to better outcomes for patients (Braithwaite et al. 2017). Positive emotions are considered a key component in building happiness and wellbeing and perhaps even preventing burnout. They could also help to promote both a positive safety culture and improve patient safety by fostering good relationships and the ability for people to speak up, listen to each other and learn from each other.

It is worth reiterating the assertion by IHI that joy in work impacts on individual staff engagement and satisfaction as well as patient experience, quality of care, patient safety and organisational performance (Perlo et al. 2017). However, if people are not convinced, is it really so bad to build structures, teams and organisations that help people experience joy in their work, help them thrive and build better relationships? The very least you can do is engage people, listening to them and finding out what their lives are like, what they need, what makes them feel safe, what makes them happy and what brings joy to their work.

4.3 Kindness and Empathy

Kindness and civility needs to be encouraged and expected. People need the opportunity to connect and FOSTER POSITIVE RELATIONSHIPS that let them be heard.

[Includes words – kindness and civility need to be encouraged and expected. People need the opportunity to connect and foster positive relationships that let them be heard]

4.3.1 Kindness

If you want to call these 'soft skills' after you've tried putting them into practice – go for it. I dare you.

Brown 2018

Kindness is the quality of being friendly, generous and considerate. It is linked to kind-heartedness, affection, warmth, gentleness, tenderness and concern. It is an unbelievable strength to be kind and not at all soft and fluffy. Sadly, when attitudes such as kindness are mentioned as a way to improve the way people work, improve the way they can do so safely and increase productivity, people roll their eyes, and as Unwin (2018) says, you are made to feel like you are 'somehow unhelpfully interrupting the adult flow of conversation'.

I think one of the saddest things about medicine is that kindness is beaten out of you to such an extent that if you have any left it is often seen as a sign of weakness.

Warriner via twitter @DrDavidWarriner 05.03.2019

Kindness is so much more than simply being nice. Kindness, including thoughtfulness, compassion and caring, enables people to be fair and professional. Kindness is a requirement of authentic and convincing leadership; it is not about being sentimental or nice. Being kind is not about avoiding hard decisions or hard conversations; it is about doing so in a way that is caring, gentle and clear, being respectful and letting the person receive the information with dignity.

Not being clear has been cited in numerous incidents and accidents.

It is kind to be clear, unkind to be unclear. This means:

■ It is kind to have the difficult conversation and provide honest feedback.
■ It is kind to talk to someone about whether their chosen specialty is the one for them or perhaps together we should find them somewhere new to work.
■ It is kind to talk to people about their competence or attitude at work.
■ It is kind to give people a way out with dignity.

Kind words can be short and easy to speak but their echoes are truly endless.

Mother Theresa

Berry and his colleagues (2017) have found that simple kindness can help to diffuse negative emotions in cancer care and that there are six types of kindness:

1. **Deep listening**, whereby clinicians take the time to truly understand the needs and concerns of patients and their families.
2. **Empathy** for the patient with cancer expressed by both individual clinicians and the care culture that seeks to prevent avoidable suffering.
3. **Generosity** – generous acts of discretionary effort that go beyond what patients and their families expect.
4. **Timely care** that is delivered by using a variety of tools and systems that reduce stress and anxiety.
5. **General honesty**, whereby the truth is conveyed directly in well-chosen guiding words.
6. **Support for family** whose physical and mental wellbeing are vital components of the care the loved ones receive.

All these are mutually reinforcing manifestations of kindness.

4.3.2 Lack of Kindness

When stress is high, we can find ourselves slipping away from kindness. Like incivility, being unkind impacts on relationships, on our ability to perform effectively, our health and wellbeing and can make people's lives intolerable. Daily acts of unkindness that we need to address include:

■ Talking behind people's backs; talking about them rather than to them
■ Feeding people half-truths or even lying to make them feel better and ourselves better
■ Not getting clear with a colleague about expectations because it is too hard and then accusing them for not delivering
■ Being rude or short

The similarities with incivility are clear. Not being kind impacts on the way people talk to and about each other, may also impact on whether people will speak up or not or perhaps worse whether they will tell the truth about what is happening in a certain situation. This could have huge implications for the safety of patients.

4.3.3 What Can We Do Differently?

We all need to be kinder, the people who make organisational decisions, the people designing policy, the media and the public – in a world of negativity, we all need to be a little bit kinder. It requires a focus on relationships and connections in a deeply human way. It is not about simply telling people what to do; it is about living the behaviour and role modelling what is the right thing to do, establishing that kindness as the way we do things around here. We can all consider the three different levels of kindness:

■ Random acts of kindness that can brighten people's day
■ Relational acts of kindness found in many one-to-one relationships
■ Radical kindness which challenges established norms

Carnegie Fellow Unwin has written a report, 'Kindness, emotions and human relationships: the blind spot in public policy' (2018), which is the result of a two-year fellowship with the Carnegie UK Trust. The report argues that the current focus on regulation, measurement and efficiency have crowded out kindness. This is echoed by Sutcliffe – CEO Nursing and Midwifery Council UK – who says 'Kindness should be at the heart of our human approach to regulation' (2019). Unwin states that some of the biggest challenges facing public policy are now about behaviour and for this to be successfully addressed it needs emotional intelligence and kindness. She cites the deep divisions in our society and the declining trust in institutions which all challenge the ways in which we work and the relationships we build. Unwin believes the case for kindness to feature in public policy is compelling as public policy needs to be fair, open to scrutiny and challenge, safe both for those who use them and those who provide them, professional and value for money. The report argues for a different way of thinking of kindness and emotion in public policy and asserts that kindness matters and without acts of kindness we would be incapable of functioning.

4.3.4 Compassion

Trzeciak, an intensivist, talks eloquently about compassion in his TED talk in 2018. His view is that we are in a 'midst of a compassion crisis'. He says that people feel that compassion is missing from today's healthcare, and that there is an epidemic of burnout of healthcare practitioners. His forthcoming book *Compassionomics* with Mazzarelli and Booker will provide further depth on this subject. It was about to be published prior to my completing this book but has already been championed by opinion leaders Berwick and Bisognano.

The talk and book provide the case for compassion as 'the wonder drug for the 21st century'. It will claim that human connection in healthcare matters in astonishing ways. The authors will demonstrate that compassion has vast benefits for patients across a wide variety of conditions, and that the missed opportunities for compassion can have devastating effects. Also, compassion can help reverse the cost crisis in healthcare and, importantly, compassion can be the antidote for the amount of burnout in healthcare providers. Trzeciak carried out research in relation to compassion and his key finding is that compassion matters for patients, for patient care and for those that care for patients and it belongs in the domain of evidence-based medicine.

4.3.5 Empathy

Empathy is an essential ingredient to support kindness and to help people appreciate and be grateful. It is not about being sympathetic or giving advice, assuming that all you need to do when someone is in distress is to tell them what to do. Empathy is not about saying 'I know how this feels because the same thing happened to me and …' People are so desperate to fix or to give advice that when someone is sharing their problems with them others chip in even before the speaker has finished. I have even done it myself. It is our human instinct to make things better; we get excited that we can help and we interrupt.

Showing empathy is not about trying to make the situation better, but it is about trying to help the person cope with the situation they are in, providing a connection and respecting the other person's perspective, connecting to the feeling of an experience rather than the experience itself. Which is why, even if you have not been bereaved or bullied or suffered from an incurable illness, you can be empathetic about the feelings that these people will be experiencing. Empathy is letting the other person know that they are not alone.

> We rarely think about how we behave in conversations, but we all know that they can feel very different depending on what we are discussing and with whom.
>
> **Wiggins and Hunter (2016)**

Wiseman (cited in Brown 2018) has identified four attributes of empathy:

- See the world as others see it.
- Be non-judgemental.
- Understand another person's feelings.
- Communicate your understanding of that person's feelings.

4.3.6 Listening

I have mentioned that key to this is to listen. Really listen. This was a key focus of my first book *Rethinking Patient Safety*. People who listen don't try to formulate a response while you are talking; they are people who hold their thoughts while you are sharing. Listening is such a simple act. It requires us to be present, and that takes practice, but often we don't have to do anything else; we don't have to advise, or coach, or sound wise, we just have to be willing to sit there and listen (Wheatley 2009).

When conversations go wrong it can lead to so many poor outcomes. Talking to each other and trying to understand another person's feelings underpins and is vital for a safety culture. An effective safe conversation needs to build on the culture of psychological safety and needs a safe, comforting and comfortable space, the time to talk, time to listen and time to observe.

> It turns out that if you change how people talk, that changes how they think
>
> **Boroditsky 2007, Professor of Psychology, Stanford University**

There is nothing more potent than being in the presence of someone who just wants to listen to you, that is, someone who is both open-minded and open-hearted; someone who does not get restless for you to find a solution or for you to take up their preferred solution. Some people find it very difficult to give up on their certainties, their positions, beliefs or self-explanations. This 'telling' approach is described by Schein in his book *Humble Inquiry: The Gentle Art of Asking Instead of Telling* (Edgar Schein 2013). Schein says we need to remove our bias towards telling, as we tell too often, and even when asking questions, we are often just telling. Each of us needs to try to unfreeze our fixed positions or move away from the entrenched views and assumptions we have long held; there is no room for high horses or grandstanding. Moving away from an attachment to a particular point of view opens us up to hear different perspectives and to shift from polarised positions or ideas. Too often people speak as if they knew already the complex situation another person is describing, and that their preferred solution developed elsewhere could be 'downloaded' and would work.

Our words are powerful; they can hurt and they can encourage. The bullying culture is extremely inhibitory; why speak up when you could get blamed or punished for doing so? Bullies can stifle conversations and shut down others in a number of ways. Telling can be a form of bullying which puts the other person down, it can imply that the other person is ignorant, it could assume that the other person does not know. People find it hard to shift from a position of advice giving to asking open and clarifying questions such as:

■ What did you notice? And what did you feel?
■ Does that happen normally?
■ How can you use that to do something differently?
■ What were others doing and saying?
■ What do you think was really going on?

Humble Inquiry is the fine art of drawing someone out, of asking questions to which you do not already know the answer, of building a relationship based on curiosity and interest in the other person.

Schein (2013)

Communicating your understanding of that person's feelings is the 'respond' part of psychological safety. A lot of communication has become one-way information sharing, or as others might say, 'simply telling or talking at'. Often people in leadership roles or in the role of an expert feel that they need to share their knowledge whether it has been asked for or not. They feel the need to demonstrate their expertise and to be 'in control' and highly directive. Even in arenas that are supposed to be about learning, the attendees are mainly being talked at with minimal time for questions and answers. People need to listen with intent to learn, or intent to understand what is being shared. You can demonstrate you are listening if you truly respond to what is being said and not with the argument or comment you wanted to say irrelevant of what is being said. Our interruptions block other people's ideas and thoughts. When people know that they won't be interrupted the meeting changes; instead of fighting for airtime, you create space to think (Heffernan 2015). This means that people will feel able to ask questions, open up if they are concerned or don't know something – all of which have been found to have contributed to things that have gone wrong in the past.

4.3.7 Kindness, Empathy and Safety

As we can see, the antidote to incivility and negative cultures is to be kind and empathetic. Being non-judgemental and understanding other people's feelings compliments both psychological safety and the restorative just culture. Kindness is the helpfulness towards someone in need, not in return for anything, but for that of the person helped. That is the very core of creating a restorative just culture.

Seeing the world as others see it and understanding other people's worlds compliments the concepts of 'Safety II' and the need to understand 'work-as-done' as well as a crucial skill for investigating both when things go wrong and when things go right. Although you cannot truly see the world as others see it because you still see it through your own eyes, you can listen to them and learn from what they say (Turner 2019). Everyone's view of the world is unique depending upon their experiences, expertise, ethnicity, cultural beliefs, and personal characteristics and so on. This is why people involved in an incident will have different perspectives from one another of what happened, why it happened and how it happened. These are their own 'truths'. Only when we get everyone's perspective will we be able to get the full picture of what went on. The challenge is to truly understand the messy reality.

An empathetic leader will learn how 'work is done' by talking to their staff, sitting down with them and listening to staff on the frontline in relation to what works and how. They then respond with acknowledging that they have understood what they have heard and clarifying this by asking them if 'this is what I heard'. It is also about acknowledging how people feel. This requires a set of values and behaviours by everyone; being kind, curious, caring, thoughtful, honest, respectful, authentic, being human, building trust, being fair, showing love and appreciation. The biggest challenge facing patient safety is the way in which people behave towards one another. Therefore, there is no doubt that kindness and empathy impact on the safety of care and can help people work safely.

4.4 Appreciation and Gratitude

Positive, joyful and kind people have a commonality, they practice gratitude (Brown 2018). Appreciation is recognition and enjoyment of the good qualities of someone or something and gratitude is the quality of being thankful; readiness to show appreciation for and to return kindness. Gratitude and appreciation are not the same as recognition or reward. They are related but not the same. Simply put, gratitude and appreciation are about feeling valued. Recognition is often related to outcomes and results (Robbins 2019).

4.4.1 Appreciation

Research has shown that, when people are recognised for what they do, they are 23% more effective; however, when they are appreciated, they are 43% more effective (Robbins 2019). Organisations across the globe are learning that recognition increases staff engagement and satisfaction by as much as 11%. A person who feels appreciated will always do more than what is expected (Gordon 2019, Robbins 2019). Feeling appreciated keeps people going when it is tough. Appreciation is needed even when things are not going so well, when it is difficult and challenging. Create an environment that appreciates people for who they are and not just what they do (Robbins 2019).

4.4.2 Gratitude

Being grateful or showing gratitude changes people. It gives you a window into your life that you might just take for granted. It is the antidote to negativity and stress. As we have seen in Part Three, incivility can deplete our immune systems and can be as bad for your health as smoking and obesity (Porath 2016). Conversely, expressing gratitude is good for your health. It lowers blood pressure and boots our immune systems (Hill, Allemand and Roberts 2013), it increases happiness and fights depression (Emmons and McCullough 2003, Sheldon and Lyubomirsky 2006, Wood Froh and Geraghty 2010) and you are more likely to be kinder to others (Bartlett and De-Steno 2006, McCullough, Kilpatrick, Emmons and Larson 2001, McCullough, Kimeldorf and Cohen 2008).

Similar to kindness, gratitude again is seen as 'fluffy' or a weakness. But people leave jobs and places when they don't feel appreciated. It may on the surface appear soft or fluffy or touchy-feely but it is far from it. If we link up positivity and joy, a prevailing sentiment in writing on happiness is that an effective approach for maximising contentment is to be consciously 'grateful for one's blessings'. Emmons et al. (2003) conducted three experimental studies and found that there is some truth to this wisdom and that there do appear to exist benefits to regularly focusing on one's blessings.

Fredrickson's (1998) broaden-and-build model of positive emotions described in Section 4.2.1 may be especially helpful in relation to gratitude. She has argued that positive emotions broaden mindsets and build enduring personal resources. Seen in the light of this model, gratitude is effective in increasing wellbeing as it builds psychological, social and spiritual resources and gratitude inspires prosocial reciprocity. The experience of gratitude, and the actions stimulated by it, build and strengthen social bonds and friendships. Furthermore, encouraging people to focus on the benefits they have received from others leads them to feel loved and cared for by others. This is one of the lovely aspects of the learning from excellence initiative described in the next section.

Therefore, gratitude appears to build friendships and other social bonds and is argued to be a form of love. To the extent that gratitude, like other positive emotions, broadens the scope of cognition and enables flexible and creative thinking, it also facilitates coping with stress and adversity. According to the broaden-and-build model, gratitude not only makes people feel good in the present, but it also increases the likelihood that people will function optimally and feel good in the future (Emmons and McCullough 2003).

4.4.3 Appreciation and Gratitude

Researchers describe a chain between appreciation and gratitude, that is, people who are appreciated are in turn grateful, then they express gratitude, then they feel appreciated and so on. There is also a theme similar to that of kindness: one act of gratitude begets another act of gratitude which begets another act of gratitude – it grows and grows (Mehta 2014).

Context is really important. It cannot be forced. However, even if people are 'told to do it', research has shown that people still enjoy it and the benefits are found to be the same (Gordon 2019). Although ultimately it is not about making it mandatory – the only reason it should be done is because you genuinely want the best for your employees. Appreciation and gratitude should not be about 'wanting anything back'. The motivation should be doing it for others not because you have to, and authenticity is vital.

How do we say thank you authentically? Gordon (2019) suggests you use the 'thank you' as an opportunity to provide a connection and share more meaningful information. Instead of simply saying thank you, expand the thank you to an explanation of why you are thankful to this person for what they did. The more specific you can be, the better. Imagine the kind of thanks you would like to receive.

There are also nuances in how it is expressed by different people and how people want to receive it. Appreciation can be offered for people who are (as some may perceive) 'just doing their job'. It can be offered when work is hard, for the times when targets are not being met, or patients are complaining or when things are going wrong. The response should be 'I know it is challenging, I know that we are not doing as well as we would like, but I appreciate that you are all working so hard and I want to thank you for that'.

It is hard to know what we might be grateful for or we might just take things we should be grateful for, for granted. If we do not recognise them, then we may not recognise the things that make us happier, healthier, kinder and more connected to others. One of the exercises Emmons and McCullough suggest is to keep a 'daily gratitude journal', writing down at least three to six things for which you are grateful every day. They suggest that doing this regularly can help you appreciate the positives in your life. To do this, think about:

- When things are going well, what does it look like?
- What does it feel like?
- What brings you joy?

It can be simply enough sleep or having time to sit for a while. Similar to the gratitude diary, you could describe what joy means to you and make a list of the things that bring you joy. You could keep a journal or make a note of what you are grateful for on your smart phone or share it with your loved ones around the kitchen table. Something as simple as starting or ending meetings with a list of things people are grateful for can build trust and connections and give people permission to be kind, feel and exhibit joy. These are genuinely lovely tips which are helpful to think about when it comes to putting gratitude in action.

4.4.4 *Appreciation, Gratitude and Safety*

Gratitude increases happiness. A person who feels appreciated will always do more than expected, and people are 43% more productive when they feel valued. This impacts on people's ability not only to be more satisfied at work, but it is also conducive to a culture of openness: it helps create connections so that people can freely raise concerns and it means that someone will notice when you need help even if that is just a hug or a cup of tea.

Grateful leaders inspire trust and are seen as having higher integrity, which energises people (Gordon 2019). If appreciated, people want to do more of the same thing. This beautifully links back to 'Safety II': if we appreciated how people are working, how they are succeeding most of the time, they will want to do more of the same thing. Given all the benefits described previously, it seems surprising that very little attention is paid to this in both healthcare and in helping people to work safely. A beautiful example of gratitude and appreciation being brought to life as part of improving safety is that of the *Learning from Excellence* initiative, which I will share with you in the next section.

4.5 Learning from Excellence

A particular component of appreciation and gratitude is to give positive and meaningful feedback. One of the ways to bring them to life is to notice the everyday acts that people do and thank them for them. This is embodied in a new initiative called *Learning from Excellence.*

4.5.1 What Is Learning from Excellence?

Learning from Excellence is a way in which people can praise others, share appreciation and gratitude for the people they work with. It was started by a group of clinicians and researchers who have a shared cause; to learn from what goes well in healthcare and to provide positive feedback to others. The pioneers are Adrian Plunkett, Emma Plunkett, Kelly, Blake and Morley.

> The principle type of learning from 'learning from excellence' is the same as the learning we experience from any type of feedback. The main difference is that it is exclusively positive feedback – an extremely rare phenomenon in today's NHS.
>
> **Adrian Plunkett 2016**

While this is a growing concept in healthcare it has gained huge traction not only in the UK but across the world. Adrian

Plunkett says that the heart of 'learning from excellence' is a 'simple, formal positive feedback tool, which allows peers to show appreciation to each other'. However, it is so much more than that: *Learning from Excellence* is a tool to highlight success and could be a key way in which 'Safety II' could be bought to life. It is about treasuring and appreciating the everyday successes, rather than taking them for granted.

The team at Learning from Excellence believe that reporting and studying success would enhance learning, improve patient outcomes and patient experience while at the same time positively impact on staff experience, resilience and a positive workplace culture. Those that receive the excellence reports are made aware of the positive effects of their actions, which gives them the opportunity to reflect and think about why their actions were so well received. As a result, people often go on to make changes in their future behaviours based on the new awareness they have of their positive actions.

4.5.2 Positive Feedback

It is really important to provide meaningful feedback for people we work with. Learning about what we do well helps for the future. Therefore, this initiative is a means of identifying and capturing learning from episodes of peer-reported excellence or positive deviance.

One of the principles of learning from excellence is that the positive feedback from each report should be privately shared with the staff member who has been reporting for excellence. This is not about overt celebration, reward or prize-giving, nor is it used to create league tables of which some areas are more positive than others. The team did not provide guidance or restrictions on which types of episode to report, leaving the reporter to apply their own definition of 'excellence'. Adrian Plunkett describes how, for him and others, providing good care every day is in of itself a form of excellence. In fact, it is not about perfectionism or striving to be outstanding or better than others.

Actually, if we think it is about perfection, then we may be setting others up to feel less than their co-workers. Brown (2018) suggests that perfectionism could hamper achievement and has been found to be correlated with depression, anxiety, addiction and missed opportunities. It does not have to be a groundbreaking innovation, just something that shows that what they did made a difference to someone else. It is about noticing the good, which can be as simple as someone making another colleague a cup of tea. It is not about the grand gesture of 'thank you' but much more a small act you can do as often as you like to show your thanks to people around you for whatever you feel they need thanks for.

4.5.3 *The Learning Part of Learning from Excellence*

To bring to life the 'learning' part of the initiative, the reports are considered at an Improving Resilience, Inspiring Success (IRIS) or Serious Incident Report Investigation (reverse SIRI) meeting. An IRIS involves a conversation between those submitting and receiving the report. This discussion uses aspects of the appreciative inquiry (AI) methodology. AI is positive, hopeful and supportive (Bushe 2013). Using a skilled facilitator and using an AI model the team are helped to understand that they can learn much more from things that go well. They can learn from their day-to-day practice in order to identify what works well, what they have achieved so far, what gets in the way of doing a brilliant job and what they could do differently in the future. The discussions take around an hour and identify how excellence was achieved, including what 'workarounds' or innovations were used. This is then used to generate ideas for sharing and promoting excellence. These meetings nurture a positive mindset and helps the gaining of new insights into moments of optimal performance.

The method helps people learn more about each other and how to pick out things they like about the way they work with each other. It also changes the way people talk to each other:

they are warm, kind and appreciative using positive words and comments. This, in turn, helps others become more confident to use positive and emotive language.

4.5.4 Other Appreciation Programmes

There are other examples of peer-to-peer appreciation programmes such as the one run by Schwab & Co. (Jason 2019), which has seen around 405,000 appreciation cards sent over the last five years. With around 15,000 employees, that is a significant number of their employees. Unlike with Learning from Excellence, the appreciation cards are not private between the sender and the receiver. Every manager gets copied on the messages, and leaders can draw reports on all of the 'sent words' or received. They are also often made part of meetings or pinned up on boards in staff areas. Appreciation and gratitude are built into the organisation induction and ongoing training programmes.

MacAleavey (2019) worked at Facebook for a while and decided to put thank-you notes in the office vending machines. She found that simply providing the opportunity and giving people the permission to say thank you was all that was needed.

4.5.5 Learning from Excellence and Safety

This initiative is demonstrating that excellence reporting can be used to support all of the concepts described in the book, bringing to life 'Safety II' and an antidote to 'Safety I', supporting the right cultures and behaviours and truly learning about the positive and joyful 'work-as-done' in order to learn how things could be replicated and strengthened. The team have also demonstrated the potential for positive effects on workplace culture and morale and potentially reducing harm in areas such as safe prescribing (Kelly 2015).

Learning from Excellence and other concepts such as AI are underpinned by the principles that learning and improvement should come from a place of understanding how things work well. It aligns beautifully with the concepts associated with positivity and positive thinking to help shift us from what we could have done differently to what would we like to continue to replicate. It supports a positive inquiry as a way of explaining what is working well through storytelling and personal experience. It is dependent upon the right set of behaviours, respect, humility, curiosity and kindness for it to work well in itself.

Part of what Learning from Excellence is trying to address is not only people wanting to share positive feedback about the people they work with; not only is it a way of thinking about what is working and how can we celebrate the fact that people are getting through their day or how people are being successful in a world that focuses on failure. It is also a serious attempt to address the balance of negative versus positive approaches to safety. As Brown says (2018), it is time to lift up our teams and help them shine.

4.6 Wellbeing

Patients are safer when those around them are PHYSICALLY, PSYCHOLOGICAL AND EMOTIONALLY WELL.

They need to be fed, supported, thanked, rewarded – even loved.

4.6.1 What Do We Mean by Wellbeing?

Wellbeing includes welfare, health, happiness, comfort and
security. It relates to both the mental and physical state. The
ability to pay attention and to be vigilant is really hard under
the best of circumstances. The forgetfulness that is a normal
human characteristic for most people combined with those who
are tired and stressed impacts significantly on safety. Issues such
as shift patterns and personal characteristics such as the meno-
pause, mental health issues, wellbeing, and conditions such as
insomnia and so on impact on memory and decision making
and, therefore, safety. We have to understand the constraints
people are under, the demands, the deadlines, the stretching
of resources, the goals and dilemmas people are faced with.
In addition, we need to understand the social and psychological factors such as the expectations of ourselves and those of
colleagues, compliance with groups, the lack of trust, the organisational culture, the incivility and the dominance of status, hierarchy and power. And finally, we need to understand how all
of this can change depending upon the people, the time of day
and the changes in the environment internally and externally.

4.6.2 Why Is It Important?

It is my view that, in addition to the attitudes and behaviours
of positivity, joy, kindness, compassion and empathy plus
appreciation and gratitude, we have to look after the wellbeing
of our staff. It is vital that their welfare, health and basic needs
are met. This means that we need to address the unacceptable
working conditions and practices that they work in. Over time,
for all sorts of reasons, the environment that staff work in has
deteriorated and areas such as common rooms, places to eat,
drink and socialise together have been slowly taken away. At
the same time, working practices and shift patterns together
with a lack of basic facilities mean that staff are experiencing
hunger and chronic fatigue.

On top of this. people are not developing the relationships needed to support their mental wellbeing and are not being simply 'cared for'. People don't seem to have the time or the energy to find out about the people they work with. Leaders don't seem to have the time or the energy to help develop their staff and build on their strengths. Time has always been one of our most precious resources, but we seem to have less and less of it. What healthcare leaders need to do is help people create dedicated time to eat, to rest, to socialise, to share things with others, to develop relationships and for people to work on things they enjoy together – helping people work well together and work things through together.

The key for attracting and retaining people is to care for people as humans. If leaders are not perceived to care or make any attempt to know about their employees and the way they work, then the workforce becomes disconnected.

Healthcare is full of people who do brave things and make brave decisions. However, compassion for staff has been eroded by the current state of healthcare, and as a result, staff are becoming isolated and lonely. If we want people to show up and continue to do their work well we need to care for them and lead them in a way that helps them do what they do every day. Kay (2017) wrote in his book *This Is Going to Hurt* that healthcare practitioners are forced to build an emotional force field around them because no one is caring for the carers. His book is heart-breaking, more because this is not the tale of one junior doctor, but a tale of so many of those who work in healthcare. Kay talks about the chronic fatigue faced by clinicians, even telling of a time when he was woken up at the traffic lights because he had fallen asleep at the wheel. He describes the way in which he was constantly late home, unable to attend special events with his loved ones, and the deep shame and grief of not being able to provide the care he would have liked to provide. The last chapter of the book left me speechless.

There is little attention paid to staff wellbeing despite even the recent *Health Education England UK Report on NHS Staff and Learners' Mental Wellbeing Commission* (Health Education England 2019) in which they set out a number of recommendations including the appointment of an NHS Workforce Wellbeing Guardian and a Workplace Wellbeing Leader in every NHS organisation. The National Health Service (NHS) in the UK has around 1 million staff who are devoted to caring for others, yet we have failed to care for them. It is no longer ok just to be grateful your staff have turned up. It is extremely important to provide a better way of caring for the people that care. It is worth, therefore, delving a little deeper into the impact of not doing so in relation to:

- Hunger
- Fatigue
- Relationships
- Psychological safety
- Loneliness and isolation

4.6.3 Hunger

A vital component of wellbeing is hydration and being fed well. This, in turn, needs adequate facilities and rest breaks. In many hospitals now, the number and quality of changing rooms have been reduced, there is a lack of 'on call' rooms and the expectation that people can work a 13-hour shift without anywhere to go and get food overnight. Many healthcare staff miss out on meals or snack high-sugar, high-fat convenience food. Little attention has been paid to ensuring that they get breaks which include getting something to eat and drink and its relationship with patient safety. Sadly, there are stories of healthcare staff being made to feel guilty for simply taking the break they are entitled to. What we do know is that people who are hungry or experiencing low blood sugar are forgetful, often angry and can be rude to the people around them and this can lead to incivility which, in turn, affects cognitive capacity and decision making, which will inevitably affect the safety of patient care.

4.6.4 Fatigue

Fatigue, exhaustion, weariness, lethargy – no matter what you call it, is a key element of basic human need and dealing with these issues vital for wellbeing, in particular for supporting health, physical and mental state. The lack of attention to this is a huge risk. Fatigue is implicated in almost every industrial accident. As a result, industries such as aviation and transport have paid attention to the fatigue of their employees for a long time because, when people fly plans or operate trains when they are fatigued, they kill people.

In healthcare, people are expected to work long hours, work through the night without a break or without even a nap. Staff are considered 'less' or 'sub-standard' if they take a break. The following quote sums it all up for me:

> The problem isn't that we can't keep working when we are tired – the problem is that we can – we just don't do it very safely.
>
> **Heffernan 2015**

Fatigue is not simply tiredness; it is a state where tiredness becomes overwhelming and isn't relieved by rest or sleep. It can be triggered or exacerbated by stress, poor diet and nutrition, lack of sleep and high-pressure working environments which usually include long working hours, sporadic short patterns, night working and lack of appropriate rest. As I mentioned, healthcare is a complex adaptive system, and in the view of those who work in resilience engineering, the people who work in healthcare need to adjust and adapt what they do in order to keep the system safe. But exhaustion and distraction as a result of fatigue can mean that people find it very difficult to respond to any changes or unexpected circumstances and take longer to reason correctly. Tired and overwhelmed, people just want the problems to go away and they don't care how because they don't have the capacity to analyse or solve them (Heffernan 2015). All people are doing is trying to get through the day.

Sleep deprivation can also lead to misunderstandings and reactions, it affects our ability to read others and judge intent. This is all bad news for civility. Inadequate sleep lowers brain glucose levels, which impairs self-regulation and self-control, which can produce more incivility (Porath 2016). Lack of sleep is damaging the workplace, with it being linked to workplace deviance, impatience and unethical behaviour. Sleepy people may also not be aware of their negative impact on others because they are just too tired to notice.

Working 11 or more hours a day at least doubles the risk of depression, and those working 55 hours a week suffer cognitive loss (Heffernan 2015). Researchers at Michigan State University have conducted the largest experimentally controlled study on sleep deprivation to date, revealing just how detrimental operating without sleep can be in everything from bakers adding too much salt to cookies to surgeons making mistakes.

> Mistakes and accidents – lack of sleep is one of the primary reasons for human error.
>
> **Stepan et al. 2018**

The research has shown that there are many people in critical professions who are sleep-deprived with nearly one-quarter of the people having fallen asleep on the job. Some basic errors, such as adding salt twice to a recipe, might not be so serious. However, some of the world's greatest human-caused catastrophes – like Chernobyl, the Exxon Valdez oil spill and the Challenger explosion – along with daily train and car accidents have sleep deprivation at least partially to blame (Stepan et al. 2018).

Sleep is critical to completing any task, be it large or small. The research suggests that sleep-deprived people shouldn't perform tasks in which they are interrupted – or, only perform them for short periods. This is really difficult in healthcare, which is full of interruptions and distractions, some of which are in fact necessary for the safety of patient care. The researchers explain that distractions we face every day, whether receiving a text message or simply answering a question, are unavoidable but especially harmful to sleep-deprived people.

The Association of Anaesthetists of Great Britain and Ireland, in coordination with the Royal College of Anaesthetists and the Faculty of Intensive Care Medicine, launched the *Fight Fatigue* campaign in 2018 to raise awareness about the impact a lack of sleep has on doctors and calls for action to change attitudes across the NHS. Dr Emma Plunkett, *Fight Fatigue* project group lead and consultant anaesthetist, at Queen Elizabeth Hospital, Birmingham, said:

> Sleep is a key part of maintaining our health and wellbeing and the issue of fatigue amongst our NHS workforce is concerning. Our Fight Fatigue campaign seeks to change attitudes across the NHS to ensure everyone understands the risks of fatigue and how to mitigate them. We hope that by collectively taking responsibility for making changes to working practice, we can improve working conditions for staff which will have a positive impact on their health and will ultimately benefit patient care.

The Association have created a checklist for staff which can be found on their website at https://www.aagbi.org/professionals/

wellbeing/fatigue/fatigue. This has been adapted for clinicians to assess fatigue and fitness to work. It asks the clinician to think about whether they have been unwell, have been exposed to risks at work, the type of medication they may be on or whether there is stress at work or home and ask if these are affecting their fitness to work. It also asks about alcohol consumption, sleep patterns and whether they have been able to eat or drink. They suggest not trying to 'power through it' as it can put the worker, colleagues and patients at risk.

There is also a fatigue tool (https://www.aagbi.org/professionals/wellbeing/fatigue/fatigue) created by the Association of Anaesthetists of Great Britain and Ireland which asks clinicians to think at the end of a shift, especially a night shift, and ask themselves some questions before they drive home. This includes asking yourself: have you slept or rested, has it been a long shift, do you rely on caffeine or energy drinks to stay awake, is there a place to sleep, do you feel tired and is it hard to concentrate? The tool suggests taking a nap before driving, and if the answers have caused concern then not to drive at all and consider other ways to get home rather than driving. In order to take a power nap prior to driving home (or any other time) the Association recommends:

- You need a quiet, dark room which is not too hot or cold.
- Ideally, find somewhere you can lie down flat.
- Ideal length is 20 minutes (10–30 minutes) – you don't want to fall into a deep sleep and have to wake up from that. Set your alarm, giving yourself a bit of time to relax first.
- Consider a small dose of caffeine before your nap; it will then be kicking in as you wake. Avoid (or reduce dose) if you need to sleep again when you get home.
- Don't worry about falling asleep; instead, think about relaxing. There are various breathing techniques and audio tools that you can try. Keep your eyes closed even if you can't sleep.

This work is similar to that of Reason's 'three buckets' (Reason 2004). As Reason says, in any given situation, the probability of unsafe acts being committed is a function of the amount of 'bad stuff' that staff are having to cope with. His model suggests 'three buckets': self, context and task.

The first bucket, 'self', relates to the current state of the individual(s) involved; the second, 'context', reflects the conditions in which the individual is working; and the third 'task' relates to the things the staff are expected to do. Self relates to things like lack of knowledge, fatigue, negative life events, inexperience, feeling under the weather, context relates to distractions, interruptions, shift handovers, harassment, lack of time, unavailability of necessary materials, unserviceable equipment and task relates to the processes, steps needed and how easy it is to do, get right or get wrong.

Reason says that full buckets (with respect to bad stuff) do not guarantee the occurrence of an unsafe act, nor do nearly empty ones ensure safety (they are never wholly empty). He and others suggest that it helps to provide some idea of probability which should lead to a conversation with others about how safe the employee feels. It is really a simple way of doing a 'rough and ready' assessment of the error risk in any given situation. Reason says that subjective ratings totalling between six and nine (each bucket has a three-point scale, rising to a total of nine for the situation as a whole) should set the alarm bells ringing.

4.6.5 *Relationships*

Healthcare is always about relationships, and those relationships are completely dependent upon people being able to talk to each other. Wheatley (2009) says, 'I believe we can change the world if we start talking to one another again' and 'change is a natural result of constructing meaning and knowledge together. If we pose the right questions and convene the conversations, one good conversation that matters could shift the direction of change forever' (Wheatley 2009).

In healthcare, teams have moved from fixed groups of individuals who work a lot together to fluid groups of people who have often not met each other or don't know each other very well. In this respect, it is essential that the ability to talk to each other is fostered as soon as possible. Introductions and a brief on 'who does what' helps, but is not enough to create a team that will trust each other, communicate effectively and be able to speak out when needed.

> Healthcare organisations do not typically facilitate relationships, integration and multidisciplinary working as a means to promote safety.
>
> **Baxter et al. 2019**

Effective teams require an understanding of the profound differences between people – their characters, personalities and how things like status and gender get in the way. Within the team there will be ideas people, there will be those that are risk averse and risk takers, there will be thinkers and the people who get things done. Within this, there needs to be a way of bringing them together so that they are all working in synergy and not against each other. If you understand this, then you realise that you can't treat all people the same – that you need to use their strengths to the team's advantage, that you may need to talk to each of them differently to make best use of their learning and working style.

Google's five-year study on highly productive teams, Project Aristotle (cited in Brown 2018), found that psychological safety – team members feeling safe to take risks and be vulnerable in front of each other – was far and away the most important of the five dynamics that set successful teams apart. Google conducted a two-year study of over 180 of their teams with the aim of finding out what drives a high-performance team and what makes up team effectiveness.

They found five dynamics that are also highly relevant for those that work in healthcare:

1. Psychological safety – people feel safe to take risks, be vulnerable in front of each other, ask questions, try new things, ask for help, learn from mistakes, challenge and speak up.This was the most important of the five dynamics.
2. Dependability – people can count on each other to get things done.
3. Structure and clarity – team members have clear goals, roles and plans.
4. Meaning of work – the work needs to be personally meaningful and important for all members of the team.
5. Impact of work – the team believe that the work matters and creates change.

4.6.6 *Psychological Safety*

Psychological safety is a shared belief that the team is safe for interpersonal risk taking without fear of negative consequences for the individual. In psychologically safe teams, members feel accepted and respected. Psychological safety arises from the fields of psychology, management, healthcare and behavioural management. Results from a number of research studies show that psychological safety plays an important role in workplace effectiveness (Edmondson 1999). It also enables teams to learn and perform.

Edmondson (1999) has been observing healthcare for years and says:

> Told to form and act as teams, most clinicians will agree with the spirit of the request but will struggle to make it happen given well documented challenges of communicating across shifts, expertise areas or hierarchical levels.

She goes on to say that what is needed is the ability to hold fast-paced conversations and to coordinate and make decisions very quickly with 'constantly shifting partners in care who don't have the luxury of forming stable well bounded teams'.

Psychological safety makes it possible to give feedback and have difficult conversations without the need to tiptoe around the truth. In psychologically safe environments, people believe that if they make a mistake, others will not penalise or think less of them for it. They also believe that others will not resent or humiliate them when they ask for help or information. This comes from when people both trust and respect each other. It produces a sense of confidence that the group will not embarrass, reject or punish someone for speaking up. Things that get in the way of psychological safety include judgement, unsolicited advice giving, interrupting and sharing outside the team meeting. Connections are vital for psychological safety: connections with people who won't judge us, people who we can talk to and people who will listen to us in the good times and the bad.

In a recent interview, Edmondson says (2019) that in 1999 she found that the most cohesive hospital teams reported making the most mistakes, not fewer. It is not that they are making more mistakes, but they are able and willing to talk about their mistakes. Since then, the research has shown that psychological safety not only makes teams perform better, but, in fact, entire organisations perform better. She believes that it is about candour: being direct, taking risks, being willing to say you have made a mistake and being willing to ask for help when you need it.

No one ever got fired for silence.

Edmondson 2019

People naturally stay safe and don't want to rock the boat, which means that they don't speak up when they could or should. Instead, what leaders need to do is, first, to show up with humility, curiosity and fallibility. Second, they need to set up meetings and sessions which make it easier for people to provide candid feedback about each other and or the organisation. Third, they need to respond. So set the stage, invite engagement and then respond (Edmondson 2019).

> What we do know is that there is an observed correlation between psychological safety and learning and performance.
>
> **Edmondson 2019**

4.6.7 Loneliness and Isolation

Many people in healthcare are working in isolation, and even when they are not working in isolation, they can feel lonely, have feelings of loneliness and isolation. An example can be found in doctors who have specialised to work in the community as general practitioners (GPs). This is a high-pressure role. GPs have to listen, assess, ask the right questions, make a diagnosis, respond and act all in around 10–15 minutes. Not only do they have clinic hours, they also have prescription reviews, telephone calls, home visits, hospital letters and ensuring records are up to date, all of which require people to work safely. The clinics are invariably full or over-running, so some key questions are:

- When do GPs get time to talk to each other?
- When do they get time to talk to the rest of the staff in the practice?
- When do they get time to talk about working safely?

One GP I spoke to said that often GPs will arrive, go into their room, see their patients and then leave – he said 'he had no idea who else worked there as he had never met them'. Working in isolation can mean that people are lying awake at night worrying about their patients, staying awake till 3 am or 4 am wondering if, as a result of being under constant pressure, they have made errors.

Many of these staff are worried about making mistakes because of tiredness and overwork. They are anxious as a result and worry if they have missed a symptom and instead of sending a patient home should have sent them to the nearest hospital (Campbell 2017). President of the Royal College of GPs, Professor Stokes-Lampard (cited in Campbell 2017) says:

■ 'GPs are professionals. We do everything we can to be meticulous; that's in our nature and is part of our training. But when you're shattered, it is possible to overlook a changed prescription request, or not update a patient's record as comprehensively as would be ideal – things that can impact on patients' health further down the line'.
■ 'But there are also more sinister things we worry about. Did I miss a symptom of something that could be more serious? If I'd had more time with that patient, would my eventual diagnosis have been different? These things play on your mind, and it isn't healthy'.

A number of GP practices are trying out different ways to tackle these factors. Local newsletters, lunchtime meetings, coffee time get-togethers and social suppers address the issues and challenges identified :

■ Time – clearly an obvious one but needs reiterating.
■ Hierarchy – a lot of practices are very hierarchical, with the most long-serving doctor as the senior partner who

has ultimate say, and then it works its way down from doctors to nurses to admin – the further down, the less of a voice they have.

- Silo working – GP practices can be structured so that the different 'groups' work in isolation of each other; GPs work on their own, nurses on their own, admin and receptionists on their own.
- There is no 'structure' or time period that creates the opportunity to talk to each other.
- The interventions often associated with conversations are designed for acute care or hospitals, such as the use of huddles, briefings and handover tools, and feel clumsy for community teams or practices.
- With the ratio targets of GP practices per population, there are increasing numbers of mergers which also has the issue of split sites – these can create challenges and barriers for getting to know people.

In other roles in healthcare, there are a lot of people who work in roles where they are considered the 'lead' person for a particular subject, including that of patient safety, and as a result think 'it is all down to them'. They feel a burden of responsibility even when they have no ability to influence. We need to connect up the people who are working separately on particular problems in isolation. People can also be isolated because of the shift work patterns and poorly functioning teams. When people and their isolated projects come together, learning increases, and instead of improving one process at a time, they improve aspects of care (and problems) that thread throughout all of these different areas. To make that a reality, we need a shared understanding of all of the moving pieces so that no single person is the connective tissue and that there is a communication process so that people can keep checking in on others. Networks are really good ways of doing this.

4.6.8 Wellbeing and the Impact on Safety

Patient safety, staff safety and staff wellbeing are for me fundamentally linked. Not attending to these aspects will impact on people's ability to work safely. In particular:

- If people are hungry or dehydrated, then we know this can affect cognitive ability, memory, mood and relationships.
- Fatigue and sleep deprivation influence the way we think, our energy levels and how we learn. It is much harder to think analytically when tired, which means that our intuition may take more control of our decisions. Deficits associated with fatigue, sleep loss and the sleepiness associated with circadian variations in alertness cannot be overcome by training or motivation.
- A lack of joy, a reduction in morale and poor psychological safety decreases the ability to build connections and relationships and teamwork.
- For both wellbeing and safety, there is a need for productive relationships between leaders and team members, between managers and clinicians and between the multidisciplinary workforces that comprise healthcare
- Organisations that struggle with wellbeing, staff recruitment and engagement will also struggle to implement 'Safety II' and the restorative just culture.

Leaders need to model caring and build connections which can only be achieved by a better understanding of what people feel and do. That means creating space and time for people to come together, creating the culture where people can tell you how things are and building a way of learning which is about the things we do well as well as the things we don't do so well. Leaders need to create spaces where people can be themselves without the crushing weight of responsibility of the work that they do. Allow them somewhere to breathe and where they can be vulnerable and where they can feel safe.

4.7 Part Four Summary

Part Four is supported by research from fields including sociology, psychology and wellbeing. I have drawn the connections between positivity, joy, kindness, empathy, appreciation and gratitude together with wellbeing and their impact on patient safety.

> Put simply, caring for the people that care is vital for building a safety culture and improving the safety of patient care.

No one can do their job safely or properly if they are exhausted or hungry or stressed. No one can do their job if there are not enough people on the same shift as them or the resources are simply not available. The only way they can do their job is if they are appreciated, valued, respected and looked after. They can do their job even better if their workplace is positive and joyful with kind and empathetic people to work with and be led by. Part Four has discovered how these attributes and qualities are really important for patient safety and presents the case for implementing this exciting, uplifting and simple way to make a difference for staff working in healthcare.

Clearly the best places to work have the best retention, and in turn, retention of staff saves a significant amount of money normally lost in recruitment costs and training new staff. However, it is more than that. Safety is directly correlated with experience gained over time and retention retains the knowledge and expertise in the organisation, the team and the individual so that again it benefits the way in which people can work safely.

'Safety I' and 'Safety II', complexity science, narrowing the gap between work-as-done and work-as-imagined integrated together with positivity, joy, kindness, gratitude, learning from excellence and caring for the people that care – all of these things make up the *optimum 'ecosystem' of safety*.

For those that say 'who has the time' or those that say 'there are no resources for this kind of work' or 'it's all just nice to do rather than what we must do', then there is a simple formula. Calculate the cost in terms of lack of productivity, performance and engagement as a result of incivility, bullying, blame disconnection, burnout and distrust and estimate the time managing all of this unproductive behaviour as well as the challenges of turnover. Then balance that with the benefits connected with positivity, positive deviants, and the increased morale associated with joy, happiness, gratitude and appreciation. Add to that the improved performance, productivity, safety and quality of the work related to kindness, empathy, appreciation and gratitude.

Therefore, leaders must invest time and resources in attending to people's health, wellbeing, psychological and physical needs or suffer the consequences in terms of cost, safety and productivity. They must do more than that; they need to live the values and behaviours they expect of others. It is not enough to say 'we have a set of values in our organisation that include kindness and respect'. They have to be lived; otherwise, they are not values at all.

> It is time to lift up our teams and help them shine.
>
> **Brown 2018**

A truly joyful and uplifting initiative is that of Learning from Excellence, which is trying to address the negative blame culture. It is a way of sharing positive feedback about the people you work with, a way of thinking about what is working and how can you can celebrate the fact that people are getting through their day or how people are being successful in a world that focuses on failure. It is a serious attempt to address the balance of negative versus positive approaches to safety.

4.8 Part Four Actions

Actions to care for the people who care:

- Model kind, positive and respectful behaviours.
- Create the conditions in which your colleagues can do the very best work they can.
- People are often reluctant to take their breaks or even to go home on time – they feel guilty if it is busy, pressured and they can see others are struggling. Sometimes they even need to be given permission to take a break or to go home at the end of their shift.
- Encourage your organisation to become an official backer of the ' Fight Fatigue' campaign.
- Set up quiet rooms for people to rest or quiet times in people's day so that they can process information and have time to think.
- Support your colleagues – respecting the importance of fatigue self-assessment and protected rest breaks is crucial to changing the culture around fatigue. Let your colleagues know that they have your support and signpost them to the *#FightFatigue* campaign hub for more information and advice.
- Talk about fatigue. Introduce the simple fatigue tool into your team's practice – it offers easy to remember mnemonics that provide a structure for supporting colleagues who may be on the brink of driving when fatigued.
- Share stories and experiences to raise awareness of the impact of fatigue.
- Value the people around you and model it from the top.
- Talk to others in the way you would like them to talk to you.
- Care about your staff, take the time to find out about them and help them build on and make the best use of their strengths.

- Set out processes in your organisation to provide positive, personal and authentic feedback.
- Use storytelling to bring it to life and build awareness – seek and share positive stories from both staff and patients.
- Give people time and space to enjoy their work – free up people's time by having meeting-free mornings or email-free days to free people up from the constant pressure to think.
- Provide the opportunity and space for people to eat together.
- Make dedicated time for colleagues, even just five minutes to share a cup of tea or your lunch.
- Create a place for people to learn more, provide information, tips, tools and help in building conversations about being thankful – make this simple to access for busy people.
- Learn new things – about your work, your patients and each other. Discovering something new is invigorating and joyful.
- Support flexibility – do your best not to micromanage your colleagues. Let their creativity and joy flourish but be available for advice and direction if needed.
- Be kind and be clear.
- Value people's input – listen to people.
- When someone shares something with you, don't rush for the solution – acknowledge what they have said and let them know that you are so glad they confided in your and that you are there to listen any time they need.
- Find someone you trust, someone who is empathetic and won't judge you and seek them out. Ask them if they can be there for you when you need it.
- When things don't go to plan, let people know that you feel for them, that they are not alone.

- Notice and capture the things you are grateful for – if they are about work then play them back to your team or your colleagues.
- Keep a gratitude diary – three to six things you are grateful for each day.
- Golden day exercise – notice and note a day when it all went amazingly.
- Ask yourself and others a series of questions – what went well today? What did we enjoy today? Who shall we thank? Who would we like to give positive and personal feedback to? What can we do to replicate this tomorrow?
- Say thank you – create a culture of positivity at the workplace by normalising thank you and you will start to hear thank yous back, e.g., set aside a part of every agenda to say thank you.
- 'Those that matter' exercise – think of someone you would like to thank, someone who has made a difference to you, or the area you work in. On a very small piece of paper write the names of those people and take ten minutes to reach out to them and share a little gratitude, for example, 'thank you for being one of the people whose opinions matter to me' or 'thank you for caring enough to be there for me'.
- Notice when people are kind to each other or making a difference, however small, to other people's lives.
- Make a note of when people around you do a great job and, importantly, how they have done this so that you can provide meaningful feedback.
- Communicate kindly and warmly in all other interactions including emails and telephone calls.
- Use positive feedback in all appraisals or reviews.
- Try it out – give someone some really lovely and positive feedback and see how it feels.

Part Five

Plant Trees You Will Never See

It's not about Safety II or even safety, really. It's bigger than that. It's about how we work. And it touches on leadership, teams, quality, safety, staff and patient experience. It's everything.

Carl Horsley 2017 via twitter @HorsleyCarl

5.1 Legacy

In *Legacy* (2013), written about the New Zealand rugby team the All Blacks, Kerr describes movingly how we are 'but a speck in the moment of time situated between two eternities, the past and the future and that true leaders are stewards of the future and they take responsibility for adding to the legacy'. This he simplifies as:

Be a good ancestor – plant trees you will never see.

Kerr 2013

Over the last two years and as my career is now in the latter part of my life I am all too well aware that our time is limited. Understanding the fragility of life is the first step in understanding our role and responsibility as leaders. I agree wholeheartedly with Kerr in that our greatest responsibility is to honour those who came before us and those who will come after and that our actions today will echo beyond our time. This book is about me leaving a legacy from all that I have learned over the last two decades. The ideas in this book are an amplification of the ideas in many other books and the minds of people who have studied safety for decades.

This book is also dedicated to my uncle, Dr Philip Woodward, because for many reasons he personifies everything the book is trying to convey. He leaves a legacy that will live long beyond his time. He was not only brilliant at everything he put his hand to and a man ahead of his time, he also epitomised the kind leadership that is needed to help people work well and safely. Being kind as a leader is to think of the little things that will make a big difference for your staff. One story comes to mind of when he was interviewing a new staff member who happened to be blind. He thought about the journey this person would be taking to get to the interview from Worcester to Malvern and worried that they may not know which stop to get off. So he decided to work out how many bridges there were in between Worcester and Malvern and realised that you can listen out for the change in ambient noise when travelling under a bridge. He then sent a note to the interviewee to let them know how many bridges there were and which number of bridges to listen out for before making their way to the train door to get out at the next station. His leadership style was one of inclusivity, curiosity and kindness. He recognised that people enjoyed learning something new and that being creative was a key way in which to tackle complicated and complex issues.

He was also at the forefront of developing relationships and bringing disparate groups together. In the 1960s, my uncle was a scientific officer at the Radar Research Establishment in Malvern. In the early days, there were a number of divisions within the establishment who like all organisations had their different groups, ideas and skills. The work that they were doing invariably had never been done before. How do you help people who have to work from a blank sheet of paper to come up with ideas and ways in which you may tackle things like getting computers to make calculations or even inter-act with their users when there is no guide book or training manual?

My uncle decided that every week the different groups should be invited to come together for tea or coffee and con-versation – they called the room the 'tea room'. They had one main rule which was to ban any conversation which con-cerned three things beginning with C; clocks, cars and com-puting. This was to rule out clocks because it was a passion of my uncle's and he knew that this would mean he would dominate the conversation. Cars, because he felt that the vast majority of the employees were men and that they would bore the minority of women who worked there with their endless details about cars. Computing, because this was, in fact, their main work-related activity and he wanted to encourage people to broaden the conversations to help learn more from and about each other but also to explore what they do in a much more creative way.

Your legacy is that which you teach.

Kerr 2013

He would pose questions that may have been triggered by the latest *New Scientist* or the most recent news but more often than not they were stimulated by some obscure question or fact. For example, one time they talked about Puccini's opera

Turandot. The opera was unfinished at the time of Puccini's death in 1924, and was completed by Franco Alfano in 1926. The question posed was; 'should an opera lover walk out at the point that Puccini stopped and before Alfano started or stay to the end?' Another question would be 'what is the centre of Malvern Hills (the nearby hills to their work) and how would you know and how many steps would it take you to walk to it? All of these things would be both fun but stimulate ideas, conversation and connections between the divisions.

I am told that my uncle embodied joy-in-work and he appreciated his staff and valued their expertise and made them feel that anything was possible. He went out of his way to create the conditions that help people work safely which include kindness, appreciation, gratitude, and fun. Successful leaders balance pride with humility. At all times he was humble and never above 'making the tea' – as Kerr (2013) says 'sweep the sheds' – i.e., never be too big to do the small things that need to be done.

A To-Do List to Leave your Legacy

- Become a leader you would like to follow. Inspire your teams to find their shared purpose, shared values, visions and beliefs.
- Your role is to 'leave the organisation or team or work in a better place'.
- Look beyond your own field to discover new approaches, learn best practices and push the margins, then they pass on what you have learned.
- As a leader be a storyteller.
- Think about the language and tone that you use; use caring, positive and supportive words.
- Role model and live the values you hold dear, focus on getting the conditions and culture right; the results will follow.
- Be humble and kind – this does not mean you are a weak leader, but the opposite – they are unbelievable strengths.

- Build trust and a way of working that encourages shared decision making and local ownership of improvements – think of your structures and consider creating a devolved structure, one that builds local ownership, autonomy and initiative.
- Create a learning environment where people can grow and develop personally and professionally – building a structured system for the development of the team, combined with a tailored map for the development of the individual.

5.2 A Call for a Movement

A social movement is a determined 'people-powered' effort to promote or resist change. When people say things like 'we must build a social movement' – we all have to realise that they cannot be forced or manipulated by central bodies or central teams. Social movements are organic and dependent upon networks, informal conversations, a shared purpose or cause and a desire for change. The leaders of social movements create the conditions for others to achieve a shared purpose (Ganz 2010). They facilitate trust, motivation and commitment and cannot be a top-down mandate.

5.2.1 Why Am I Talking about Social Movements?

The health service is full of 'must dos'; alerts, guidance, standards, interventions, initiatives, targets and rules. History has shown us that central commands are only likely to be complied within the short term and often fail to embed changes in the long term. They lead people to feel intense pressure to comply with a set of priorities that are not the same set of priorities that are important to them. The expected interventions move individuals and organisations away from their own priorities and also inhibit the development of local knowledge and ownership of safety. By not telling people what to do you in fact energise them; surprise them and people find this really exhilarating.

Social movements are completely different from this traditional model. They are all about role modelling and living values; building a culture of respect and kindness. There is no ordering people to do stuff or telling people that they have to be respectful and kind but instead being respectful and kind. Social movements ask 'how can I help all these people do what they want to do? Social movements are about 'changing the world, not yearning for it, or just thinking about it' (Ganz 2010)

There are four modes of change described by Russell (2018):

- The TO mode which is when change is done to us, without us.
- The FOR mode which is when change is done for us, without us.
- The WITH mode which is when change is done for us, with us.
- The BY mode which is when change is done by us, for us.

The last one, the BY mode is the one you should be seeking. A movement will provide you with the power to do that. Russell helps us by providing ways to expand the BY space – and create the possibility for more bottom-up change – he suggests the following questions to ask:

What would you love to do if three of your colleagues were willing to help?

What do we care about enough to take action on?

What are the things that we can do – or should do – to create change?

What would it take to get others involved?

What are the things that we can lead and achieve with the
   support of management or others?

What gifts (things you were born with), skills (things you
   have practised/learned to do), and passions (things you
   care about and are acting on or want to act on) could we
   tap into to address and realise our dreams, or address the
   concerns we have?

What will we do, stop doing, or not do, that will help to
   discover and enlarge free space, which can be used for
   change by staff?

5.2.1.1 Why a Social Movement for Safety?

Safety is everybody's business. It is not the role of the Head
of Patient Safety or the patient safety team. When we reframe
patient safety to working safely not only does it change the
mindset; it shifts it from a few people's job to everyone's.
Working safely is about everything. This shared purpose and
responsibility should be at the heart of a social movement for
safety. Shared responsibility means shared ownership. A sense
of inclusion and belonging means individuals are more willing
to give themselves to a common cause. This is what a social
movement is all about.

Change to the way we do safety has to grow from the
grassroots – it needs to be emergent rather than forced. At the
same time, it needs to be organised and lead. However, not in
a top-down, must do kind of leadership. It needs a distributed
leadership approach which recognises that everyone has unique
skills and something different to add to the team. Safety strategies need to be long-term aims and not short-term projects. It
needs to evolve and take its time – this is not about a short-
term spark or massive transformation. Think of it as a century
and half of evolution, building on the learning from those early
pioneers. So, do justice to the learning from Nightingale and
Semmelweiss, pick up the clues from the early days of studying
harm and link that with the learning we have today.

We all want purpose; a meaningful life. If we view safety as the variety of individual members of an orchestra; all experts in their own fields then who is the conductor? Is that you? Can you bring these people together to make a better sound? What is the drum beat of the orchestra?

Healthcare staff can build a 'social movement' to change the direction of safety from one that focuses on failure to one that looks at failure and success equally in order to help people work safely. The solidarity of collaborating with others in a common cause energises us. In particular, we can use social movement principles to create local ownership and self-direction. Everyone whether providing healthcare, monitoring, inspecting, guiding or commissioning, could be part of this social movement to provide a positive purpose, hope and energy that inspires rather than crushes. Hope is what allows us to deal with problems and is one of the most precious gifts we can give each other and the people we work with (Ganz 2010). Key to achieving this is being positive, personalised and telling stories with optimism. Stories of powerful personal narratives of individual learning can inspire people to keep going. They are not a set of messages or sound bites. Stories that demonstrate how staff are implementing their plans, stories to illustrate the impact of local activity for safety, stories about how they overcame a challenge and stories of possibility. Stories can make a significant contribution to personal and professional growth as they communicate our values through the language of the heart; our emotions (Ganz 2009).

Social movements can still include leaders. In fact, they are even better if there are leaders as part of the community with a shared purpose as over time movements need to be organised. Leaders can help create a movement that also helps deliver the shared purpose. Surprisingly, after a while, social movements require specific actions with real deadlines (Ganz 2010). Without this, the initial spark will simply die down and become a distant memory. These actions need careful thought, one of the main reasons movements are not committed to them is the fear of demotivating the people who think the movement has turned into a 'must do' task. Being organised reminds people what needs to be done, what's important and what will happen next. This requires a balance which avoids both micromanagement and hands off management (Ganz 2010). A social movement requires clarity in purpose, one that speaks to people's values, attracts them to want to (even demand) change. The clarity of purpose for me is to shift our approach to safety to one that is far more positive and balanced, that really addresses the negative and punitive culture we have today and cares for the people that care. Leaders across the NHS could inspire people to change and work differently.

5.2.1.2 What Can You Do?

The time is right for us to inspire a social movement for safety for future generations and beyond because:

- A movement can show the value of saying thank you to the people around you, value and appreciate them, and care for the people that care.
- A movement of people can shift us away from the pure focus on failure to one of balancing failure and success to achieve safety.
- A movement of people can help address the blame culture and incivility and help people talk to each other.

Be part of this movement, grow a community around you and motivate them to use the concepts and ideas shared with you. There is a moral imperative to support our staff. Run a campaign for safety – the most effective way to organise the most valuable resource of time. Campaigns are strategic and motivational ways to target effort and organise change activity; it provides a rhythm for others to follow. They unfold over time with a rhythm that slowly builds foundation and gathers gradual momentum with a few peaks along the way. A good campaign can be thought of as a symphony of multiple movements that adapts to the rhythm of change (Ganz 2010).

Develop relationships and friendships and spread the messages as you go along. People are desperate for hope and to a move away from the relentless negativity to a more positive interpretation of safety and you can do that for them. Have the courage to do it differently. Change the language, tone and conversation from the pure focus on the negativity and failure and share the factual optimistic view of positive safety and success. Share the stories and the facts that provide us with hope that things are getting better and that we can achieve more.

5.3 Conclusion

The Mind, Once Stretched by a New Idea, Never Regains Its Original Dimensions.

Oliver Wendell Holmes

This book started by exploring the latest thinking in safety and asked 'why is healthcare not safer as a result of all of the work we have done to date under the heading of "patient safety"'? I started by drawing from all sorts of other sciences and concepts and my first realisation was that those that work in safety in healthcare need to think differently about how safety is positioned and how we need to look at success as much as failure. It is time to get beneath the surface of the superficial approach to safety.

The second realisation was that there were relatively simple and extremely useful methods for understanding how we can study work-as-done and the adjustments and adaptations people make every day. The third realisation was that relationships, connections between people and friendships are crucial for helping people to work safely. This was at the same times as I appreciated that the way in which we work in healthcare, the rudeness, bullying and inappropriate behaviours were eroding these relationships and connections.

However, the most important realisation is that in order to improve or maintain patient safety we cannot simply focus on patient safety. We have to focus on how we work and the values and conditions that help us work. How we work together, how we lead, how we talk to one another and develop not only relationships but friendships, how we make decisions, how we cope with our daily dilemmas, how we adjust and adapt every day and, most importantly, how we behave. There are some key things that help people work safely; culture, values, attributes, qualities, behaviours and conditions which help people build relationships and forge connections and help them to work together. My work over the last two years has taken an unexpected journey. I had no idea that I would study joy, positivity, kindness, empathy, appreciation and gratitude and wellbeing to help me think about how care could be safer. The phrase that summed up this work was that we need to 'care for the people that care'.

I have talked to thousands of people about our concepts and ideas and without fail the recipients say how much it resonates with their everyday, how finally they feel that someone is listening, hearing them and understanding what they are feeling. This has resulted in the themes discussed here and the resultant suggested actions to implement a new approach to patient safety; create a balanced approach to safety, urgently tackle the blame culture and care for the people that care.

Crucially, it is the combination of everything within the book rather than attending to each of the parts in isolation. This is not a step by step process, it is not linear and most definitely there is no 'one thing' or 'silver bullet'. Not only is there no 'one thing', there is also no quick fix way of doing this. While that sounds negative, actually it is a positive, it frees people up from the transient and short-term attempts to improve the safety of patients to realise that they can take their time to help people work safely for future generations and beyond.

> The world we live and work in is complex so the notion of a single approach to patient safety must be rejected.

And finally, as Kerr in his book about the All Blacks, *Legacy* (2013) says; I have sought to be a good ancestor and to plant trees I will never see as I am 'but a speck in the moment of time situated between two eternities, the past and the future'. Kerr beautifully states that 'true leaders are stewards of the future and they take responsibility for adding to the legacy'. It is, therefore, my hope that the work of *Sign up to Safety* and this book has added to the legacy of work in relation to safety and that our actions over the last five years in particular will echo beyond our time.

That just leaves me to say, thank you so much for reading the book – all I ask of you now is that you take your open hearts and minds and help build the social movement for patient safety so that you too can be a good ancestor and plant trees you will never see.

References

Amalberti R, Vincent C, Auroy Y et al. (2006) Violations and migrations in health care: a framework for understanding and management. *BMJ Quality and Safety 15*, i66–i71.

Anonymous (2018) I'm the GP being sued for missing your devastating diagnosis. I'm so sorry. https://www.theguardian.com/society/2018/nov/15/gp-sued-missing-devastating-diagnosis-sorry.

Ariely D (2012) *The Honest Truth about Dishonesty*. London, UK: Harper Collins Publishers.

Bartlett MY, De-Steno D (2006) Gratitude and prosocial behaviour: Helping when it costs you. *Psychological Science 17*, 319–325.

Baxter R, Taylor N, Kellar I, Lawton R (2019) A qualitative positive deviance study to explore exceptionally safe care on medical wards for older people. *BMJ Quality and Safety.* doi:10.1136/bmjqs-2018-008023.

Berry L, Danaher TS, Chapman RA, Awdish RLA (2017) Role of kindness in cancer care. *Journal of Oncology Practice 13*(11), 744–750. doi:10.1200/JOP.2017.026195.

Berwick D (2019) In conversation at the Institute of Healthcare Improvement Quality Conference in Glasgow March 2019 via youtube.com.

Braithwaite J, Herkes J, Ludlow K, Testa L, Lamprell G (2017) Association between organisational and workplace cultures, and patient outcomes: Systematic review. *BMJ Open 7*, e017708. doi:10.1136/bmjopen-2017-017708.

Brennan TA, Leape LL, Laird NM (1991) Incidence of adverse events and negligence in hospitalized patients: Results of the Harvard medical practice study. *New England Journal of Medicine 324*(6), 370–384.

Briant R, Buchanan J, Lay-Yee R, Davis P (2006) Representative case series from New Zealand public hospital admissions in 1998–III: Adverse events and death. *New Zealand Medical Journal 119*, U1909.

Brown B (2018) *Dare to Lead*. London, UK: Vermilion.

Boroditsky, L (2017) *How Language Shapes the Way we Think* via TEDWomen.ted.com

Bushe GR (2013) The appreciative inquiry model. In EH Kessler (ed.) *Encyclopedia of Management Theory* (Volume 1, pp. 41–44). London, UK: Sage Publications.

Campbell D (2017) GPs losing sleep over patient safety fears, says head of profession. *Guardian*. https//www.theguardian. com.

Carthey J, Walker S, Deelchand V, Vincent C, Harrop Griffiths W (2011) Breaking the rules: Understanding non-compliance with policies and guidelines. *BMJ 343*, d5283. doi:1136/bmj. d5283.

Catchpole K (2013) Spreading human factors expertise in healthcare: untangling the knots in people and system. *BMJ Quality and Safety 22*(10), 793–797.

Cawsey MJ, Ross M, Ghafoor A, Plunkett A, Singh A (2018) Implementation of learning from excellence initiative in a neonatal intensive care unit. *ADC Fetal & Neonatal,* May; 103(3): F293. http://dx.doi.org/10.1136/archdischild -2017-314737.

Department of Health (2000) *An Organisation with a Memory*. London, UK: The Stationary Office.

Dekker S (2010) *Just Culture: Balancing Safety and Accountability* 2nd Edition. Aldershot, UK: Ashgate Publishing Limited.

Dekker S (2018) I am not a policy wonk. Blog via www.safetydiffer-ently.com

Dekker S (2019) A restorative just culture checklist via www. sidneydekker.com

De Vos MS (2018) Healthcare improvement based on learning from adverse outcomes. PhD thesis via twitter @maritsdv and www. reader.ogc.nl Leiden University Medical Center.

Edmondson AC (1999) Psychological safety and learning behavior in work teams. *Cornell University Administrative Science Quarterly 44*, 350–383.

Edmondson AC (2019) Creating psychological safety in the workplace the HBR IdeaCast via www.hbr.org

Emmons RA, McCullough ME (2003) Counting blessings versus burdens: An experimental investigation of gratitude and subjective wellbeing in daily life. *Journal of Personality and Social Psychology 84*, 377–389.

Eurocontrol (2006) Revisiting the Swiss Cheese Model of Accidents EEC Note No 13/06 Project Safbuild. European Organisation for the Safety of Air Navigation.

Eurocontrol (2017) Just culture definition via https://www.eurocontrol.int/articles/just-culture.

Fredrickson B (1998) What good are positive emotions? *Review of General Psychology 2*, 300–319.

Fredrickson B (2000) Cultivating positive emotions to optimise health and wellbeing. *Prevention and Treatment 3*(1). doi:10.1037/1522-3736.3.1.31a.

Fredrickson B (2001) The role of positive emotions in positive psychology: The broaden and build theory of positive emotions. *American Psychologist 56*(3), 218–226.

Fredrickson B (2004) The broaden and build theory of positive emotions. *Philosophical Transaction of the Royal Society B 359*, 1367–1377.

Fredrickson B (2013) Positive emotions broaden and build. In Patricia Devine and Ashby Plant (eds.) *Advances in Experimental Social Psychology* (Volume 47, pp. 1–53). Amsterdam: Elsevier.

Furniss D, Curzon P, Blandford A (2019) Using FRAM beyond safety: A case study to explore how sociotechnical systems can flourish and stall via http://discovery.ucl.ac.uk/1474989/1/FRAM%20PositiveResonance%20PrePrint.pdf

Ganz M (2010) Leading change. In N Nohria, R Khurana (eds.) *Handbook of Leadership Theory and Practice* (pp. 1–45). Boston, MA: Harvard Business Press.

Garrett S (2019) in conversation with the author.

Glouberman S, Zimmerman B (2002) Complicated and complex systems: What would successful reform of medicare look like?. Commission on the Future of Health Care in Canada: Discussion Paper No. 8. via https://www.researchgate.net/profile/Sholom_Glouberman/publication/265240426_Complicated_and_Complex_Systems_What_Would_Successful_Reform_of_Medicare_Look_Like/links/548604670cf268d28f044afd/Complicated-and-Complex-Systems-What-Would-Successful-Reform-of-Medicare-Look-Like.pdf?origin=publication_detail.

Gordon A (2019) Four myths about being grateful at work
via https://greatergood.berkeley.edu/video/item/
four_myths_about_being_grateful_at_work.

Gupta K, Lister S, Rivadeneira NA, Mangurian C, Linos E, Sarkar
U (2018) Decisions and repercussions of second victim
experiences for mothers in medicine. *Quality and Safety in
Healthcare.* doi:10.1136/bmjqs-2018-008372.

Health Education England (2019) NHS Staff and Learners' Mental
Wellbeing Commission via https://www.hee.nhs.uk/sites/
default/files/documents/NHS%20%28HEE%29%20-%20
Mental%20Wellbeing%20Commission%20Report.pdf.

Heffernan M (2015) *Beyond Measure: The Big Impact of Small
Changes.* New York: Simon & Schuster.

Hickson GB, Moore IN, Pichert JW, Benegas Jr M (2012) Chapter
1: Balancing systems and individual accountability in a safety
culture. In S Berman (ed.) *From Front Office to Front Line*,
2nd ed. (pp. 1–36). Oakbrook Terrace, IL: Joint Commission
Resources.

Hill PL, Allemand M, Roberts BW (2013) Examining the pathways
between gratitude and self-rated physical health across adult-
hood. *Personality and Individual Differences 54*, 92–96.

Hogan H (2016) The problem with preventable deaths. *BMJ
Quality and Safety 25*(5), 320–323. doi:10.1136/bmjqs-
2015-004983.

Hogan H, Healey F, Neale G, Thomson R, Vincent C, Black
N (2012) Preventable deaths due to problems in care in
England acute hospitals: A retrospective case record review
study. *BMJ Quality and Safety 21*, 737–745. doi:10.1136/
bmjqs-2011-001159.

Hogan H, Zipfel R, Neuburger J, Hutchings A, Darzi A, Black N
(2015) Avoidability of hospital deaths and association with
hospital-wide mortality ratios: Retrospective case record review
and regression analysis. *BMJ 351*, h3239. doi:10.1136/bmj.
h3239.

Hollnagal E (2012) A tale of two safeties. www.reslienthealthcare.
net.

Hollnagel E (2014) Is safety a subject for science? *Safety Science 67*,
21–24. http://dx.doi.org/10.1016/j.ssci.2013.07.025.

Hollnagel E (2016) Philosophical Breakfast Club presentation via
www.thephilosophicalbreakfastclub.org.uk.

Hollnagel E (2017) Can we ever imagine how work is done? HindSight *25* Summer 2017 via https://www.eurocontrol.int/ sites/default/files/publication/Hindsight/hindsight-25-from-the-briefing-room-1.pdf.

Hollnagel E, Braithwaite J, Wears RL (2013) *Resilient Health Care.* Farnham, Surrey, UK: Ashgate Publishing Limited.

Hollnagel E, Hounsgaard J, Colligan L (2014) *FRAM – The Functional Resonance Analysis Method – A Handbook for the Practical Use of the Method* via http://functionalresonance.com/ onewebmedia/FRAM_handbook_web-2.pdf

Huxley E (1975) *Florence Nightingale.* London, UK: Chancellor Press.

Iedema R, Mesman J, Carroll K (2013) *Visualizing Health Care Practice Improvement: Innovation from Within.* Boca Raton, Florida: CRC Press.

Jason D (2019) Do gratitude programs really make a difference at work via https://greatergood.berkeley.edu/video/item/ do_gratitude_programs_really_make_a_difference_at_work.

Kahneman D (2012) *Thinking, Fast and Slow.* London, UK: Penguin Random House.

Kaleidoscope Healthcare (2018) Beyond Burnout via http://www. kaleidoscope.healthcare/uploads/8/0/2/1/80213224/beyond_ burnout.pdf.

Kay A (2017) *This is Going to Hurt – Secret Diaries of a Junior Doctor.* Basingstoke, UK: Picador.

Kerr J (2013) *Legacy: What the All Blacks Can Teach Us About The Business of Life.* London, UK: Constable/Little Brown.

Kelly N, Blake S, Plunkett A (2015) Learning from excellence in healthcare: A new approach to incident reporting via https:// learningfromexcellence.com/.

Kline R (2018) NHS Bullying isn't just toxic for staff: Its costing billions. *Guardian* via www.theguardian.com.

Lawton R, Taylor N, Clay-Williams R, Braithwaite J (2014) Positive deviance: A different approach to achieving patient safety. *BMJ Quality and Safety 23*, 880–883. doi:10.1136/ bmjqs-2014-003115.

Learning from Excellence – Resources are freely available online at http://www.learningfromexcellence.com. Learning from Excellence Blogs found via http://learningfromexcellence. com/blog/.

Lilford R (2017) Implementation science at the crossroads. *BMJ Quality and Safety* – published online accessed 2 April 2019. doi:10.1136/bmjqs-2017-007502.

Lilford R, Pronovost P (2010) Using hospital mortality rates to judge hospital performance: A bad idea that just won't go away. *BMJ 340*, c2016. doi:10.1136/bmj.c2016.

MacAleavey K (2019) How to create a workplace where people feel appreciated via https://greatergood.berkeley.edu/video/item/how:to_create_a_workplace_where_people_feel_appreciated.

Macrae C (2016) The problem with incident reporting. *BMJ Quality and Safety 25*, 71–75. doi:10.1136/bmjqs-2015-004732.

Mannion R, Braithwaite J (2017) False dawns and new horizons in patient safety research and practice. *International Journal of Health Policy and Management 6*(12), 685–689. doi:10.15171/ijhpm.2017.115.

Marx D (2016) *Dave's Subs: A Novel Story about Workplace Accountability* (Video file). Eden Prairie, MN: By Your Side Studios.

McCullough ME, Kilpatrick SD, Emmons RA, Larson DB (2001) Is gratitude a moral affect? *Psychological Bulletin 127*, 249–266.

McCullough ME, Kimeldorf MB, Cohen AD (2008) An adaptation for altruism: The social causes, social effects and social evolution of gratitude. *Current Directions in Psychological Science 17*, 281–285.

Mehta N (2014) Making gratitude viral via https://greatergood.berkeley.edu/video/item/making_gratitude_viral.

Mesman J (2016) *Exnovation* via Australian Institute of Health Innovation Seminar Series at the Macquarie University. YouTube found at https://www.youtube.com.

Munro J (2018) What's the use of positive stories? Blog from Care Opinion via www.careopinion.org.uk.

NHS Improvement (2018) Never events policy and framework. www.improvement.nhs.uk/documents/2265/Revised_Never_Events_policy_and_framework_FINAL.pdf.

Perlo J, Balik B, Swensen S, Kabcenell A, Landsman JFD (2017) IHI Framework for Improving Joy in Work. Cambridge Massachusetts via www.ihi.org/resources/pages/. IHIWhitePapers/Framework-Improving-Joy-inWork.aspx

Pinker S (2016) *The Surprising Decline in Violence* TED2007 via www.ted.com.

Pinker S (2017) *Chris Anderson Interviews Steven Pinker* via TED talks via www.ted.com.

Plsek P, Greenhalgh T (2001) The challenge of complexity in healthcare. *British Medical Journal. 323*(7313), 625–8.

Plunkett A (2016) Learning from excellence - conference talk via https://swahsn.com found on youtube.com.

Plunkett A (2019) How do we know this works? https://learningfromexcellence.com/.

Porath C (2016) *Mastering Civility: A Manifesto for the Workplace.* New York: Grand Central Publishing.

Porath C, Pearson C (2013) The price of incivility. *Harvard Business Review 91*(1–2), 114–121, 146.

Quercia D (2015) Happy maps via https://thepsychologist.bps.org.uk/volume-28/march-2015/happy-maps and via TED talks https://www.ted.com/talks/daniele_quercia_happy_maps.

Reason J (2004) Beyond the organisational accident: the need for error wisdom on the frontline. *Quality and Safety in Healthcare 13* (Supple II): ii28–ii33. doi 10.1136/qshc.2003.009548.

Riordan CM (2013) We all need friends at work *Harvard Business Review* via https://hbr.org/2013/07/we-all-need-friends-at-work.

Riskin A, Erez A, Foulk TA, Kugelman A, Gover A, Shoris I, Riskin KS, Bamberger PA (2015) The impact of rudeness on medical team performance: A randomized trial. *Pediatrics 136*(3), 487–495.

Robbins M (2019) Why we need appreciation (not just recognition) at work [Video file] *Greater Good Magazine* via https://greatergood.berkeley.edu/video/item/why_we_need_appreciation_not_just_recognition_at_work.

Russell C (2018) Four modes of change: to, for, with, by. *HindSight 28* via https://www.eurocontrol.int/sites/default/files/publication/files/HindSight28.pdf.

Schein E (2013) *Humble Inquiry: The Gentle Art of Asking Instead of Telling.* San Francisco, CA: Berrett-Koehler.

Shorrock S (2013) Why do we resist new thinking about safety and systems. Blog via humanisticsystems.com.

Shorrock S (2017) The varieties of human work. Blog via https://humanisticsystems.com/2016/12/05/the-varieties-of-human-work/.

Sheldon KM, Lyubomirsky S (2006) How to increase and sustain positive emotion: The effects of expressing gratitude and visualising best possible selves. *The Journal of Positive Psychology 1*, 73–82.

Stepan ME, Fenn KM, Altmann EM (2018) Effects of sleep deprivation on procedural errors. *Journal of Experimental Psychology: General.* doi:10.1037/xge0000495.

Sutcliffe A (2019) Professional regulation and kindness. Blog via https://www.nmc.org.uk/news/news-and-updates/category/Andrea%20Sutcliffe%27s%20blog/.

Trzeciak S (2018) *How 40 Seconds of Compassion Could Save a Life* [Video file] TEDxPenn via youtube.com.

Turner C (2019) Quote from conference presentation 15 March 2019 – Patient Safety Conference at University of Birmingham.

Unwin J (2018) Kindness, emotions and human relationships: The blind spot in public policy. *Carnegie UK Trust.* https://www.carnegieuktrust.org.uk/publications/kindness-emotions-and-human-relationships-the-blind-spot-in-public-policy/.

Vincent C, Amalberti R (2016) *Safer Healthcare: Strategies for the Real World.* New York: Springer Open.

Vincent C, Burnett S, Carthey J (2013) *The Measurement and Monitoring of Safety.* London, UK: The Health Foundation.

Vincent C, Burnett S, Carthey J (2014) Safety measurement and monitoring in healthcare: A framework to guide clinical teams and healthcare organisations in maintaining safety. *BMJ Quality and Safety I Healthcare 23*(8), 670–677.

Wears RL, Hollnagel E, Braithwaite J (2015) *Resilient Health Care, Volume 2: The Resilience of Everyday Clinical Work.* Farnham, UK: Ashgate Publishing Ltd.

Wheatley M (2009) *Turning to One Another; Simple Conversations to Restore Hope for the Future.* San Francisco, CA: Berrett-Koehler Publishers Inc.

Wiggins L, Hunter H (2016) *Relational Change.* London, UK: Bloomsbury Publishing.

Wong G (2015) And now for something completely different. Blog via www.gswong.com.

Wong G (2018) Safety differently: Recipe follower and or chef? Blog via www.gswong.com.

Wood AM, Froh JJ, Geraghty AW (2010) Gratitude and well-being: A review and theoretical integration. *Clinical Psychology Review 30*, 890–905.

Woodward S (2008) From information to action: Improving implementation of patient safety guidance in the NHS. DProf thesis, Middlesex University [Online]. Available at http://eprints.mdx.ac.uk/6920/.

Woodward S (2017) *Rethinking Patient Safety*. New York: CRC Press.

Zegers M, de Bruijne MC, Wagner C, et al. (2009) Adverse events and potentially preventable deaths in Dutch hospitals: Results of a retrospective patient record review study. *Quality and Safety Health Care 18*, 297–302. doi:10.1136/qshc.2007.025924.

Index